The MAILBOX®

Kids in the Kitchen

MW00669177

MAGAZINE

Preschool–Kindergarten

The best "Kids in the Kitchen" recipes from the 1996–2007 issues of *The Mailbox*® magazine

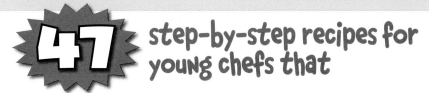

47 step-by-step recipes for young chefs that

- **connect to popular themes**

- **provide practice with following directions**

- **reinforce early reading skills**

- **require limited teacher prep**

- **are superfun to make and eat**

Editorial Team: Becky S. Andrews, Diane Badden, Kimberley Bruck, Karen A. Brudnak, Pam Crane, Pierce Foster, Tazmen Hansen, Marsha Heim, Lori Z. Henry, Debra Liverman, Kitty Lowrance, Jennifer Nunn, Mark Rainey, Hope Rodgers, Tina Petersen, Rebecca Saunders, Rachael Traylor, Sharon M. Tresino, Zane Williard

www.themailbox.com

©2010 The Mailbox® Books
All rights reserved.
ISBN10 #1-56234-905-8 • ISBN13 #978-1-56234-905-9

Printed in the United States
10 9 8 7 6 5 4 3 2 1

HPS 213549

TABLE OF CONTENTS

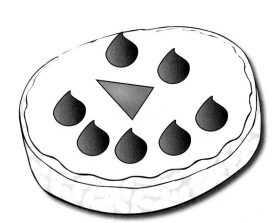

WHAT'S INSIDE

For each recipe

Step-by-step direction cards

Details for the teacher

Bear Pawprint

Ingredients for one:
graham cracker square
1 tbsp. whipped topping
chocolate cookie
5 mini chocolate chips

Utensils and supplies:
small paper plate for each child
measuring tablespoon
plastic knife for each child

Teacher preparation:
- Arrange the supplies and ingredients for easy student access.
- Display the recipe cards from page 159. Or give each student a copy of page 158, then ask her to color and cut apart the booklet pages and staple them in order.

adapted from an idea by Michelle Miles, Early Childhood Development Center, Charlottesville, VA

157

Bear Pawprint

TEC61214   1

Put one.   2

Measure.   3

Spread.   4

Put one.   5

Put five.   6

Put at snack-making center

Bear Pawprint

Name _____ TEC61214   1

Put one.   2

Whipped Topping   Measure.   3

Spread.   4

Put one.   5

Put five.   6

Send home for at-home preparation

Request for ingredients

Dear Parent,
    We are making a **Bear Pawprint** snack soon. We would be grateful if you could help by providing the following ingredient(s):

_____

_____

We need the ingredient(s) listed above by _____ date

Please let me know if you are able to send the ingredient(s).
          Thank you,

_____
          teacher

Bear Pawprint

☐ Yes, I am able to send the ingredient(s).
☐ No, I am unable to send the ingredient(s) this time.

_____
          parent signature

The Best of The Mailbox® Kids in the Kitchen • ©The Mailbox® Books • TEC61214

Comments from the chef

I Made a Bear Pawprint in School Today!

My favorite part was _____.

It tasted _____.

This is what it looked like:

Chef's signature: _____

The Best of The Mailbox® Kids in the Kitchen • ©The Mailbox® Books • TEC61214

School Bus Snack

Ingredients for one:

graham cracker (4 sections)
yellow-tinted soft cream cheese
4 pieces of Chex cereal
2 Mini Oreo cookies

Utensils and supplies:

paper plate for each child
plastic knife for each child

Teacher preparation:

- Arrange the supplies and ingredients for easy student access.
- Display the recipe cards from page 7. Or give each student a copy of page 6; then ask him to color and cut apart the booklet pages and staple them in order.

Melissa Hauck—Grs. PreK–1, Pear Tree Point School, Darien, CT

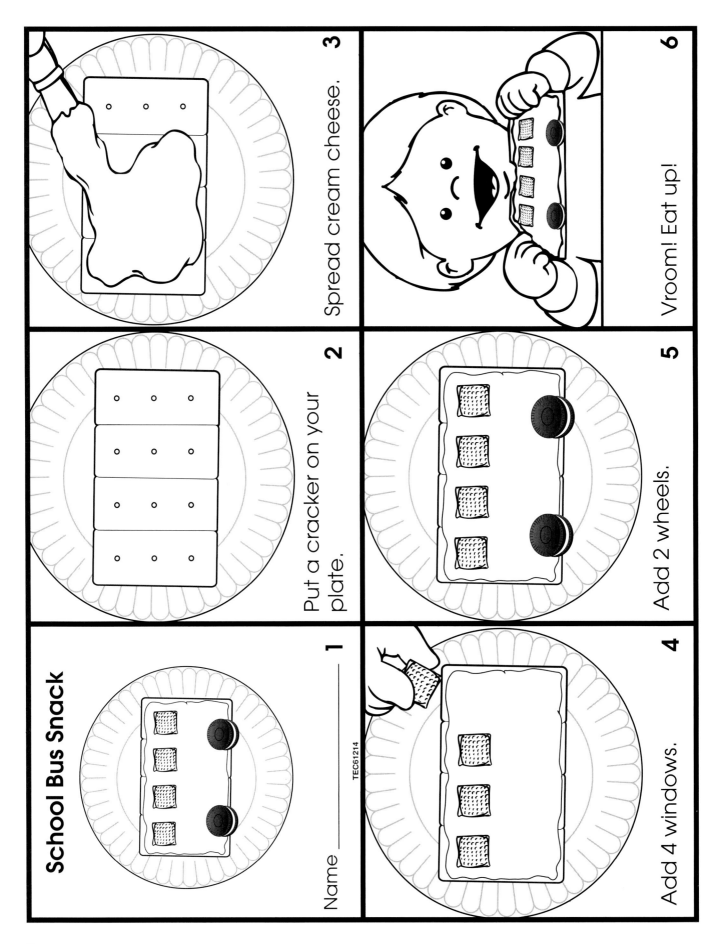

School Bus Snack

Name _____

TEC61214

1

2

Put a cracker on your plate.

3

Spread cream cheese.

4

Add 4 windows.

5

Add 2 wheels.

6

Vroom! Eat up!

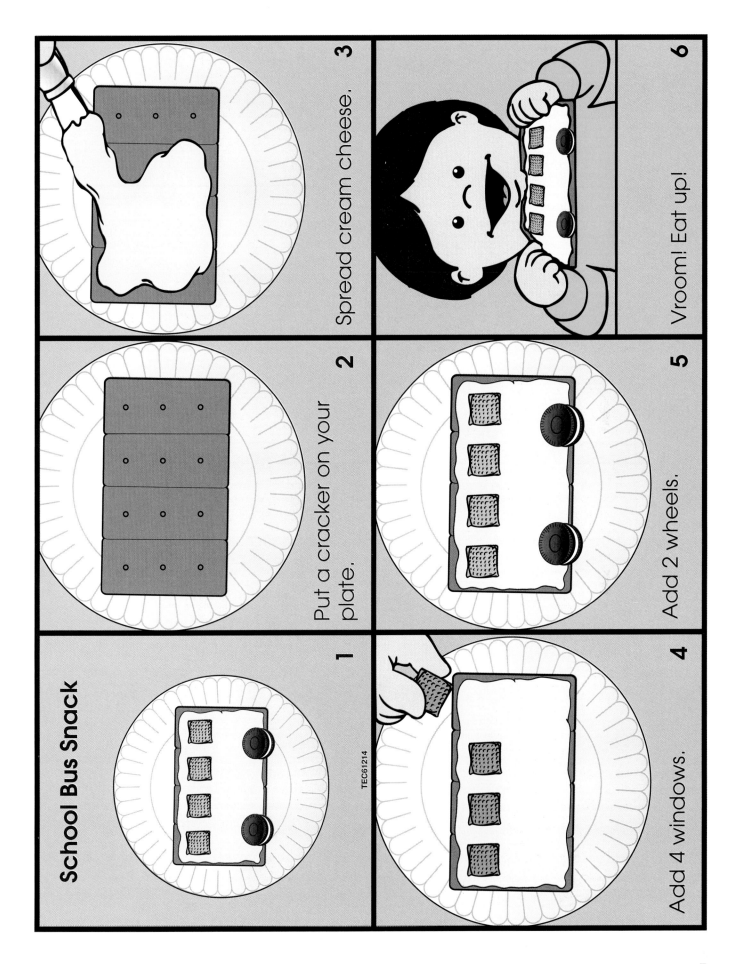

School Bus Snack

1

2 Put a cracker on your plate.

3 Spread cream cheese.

4 Add 4 windows.

5 Add 2 wheels.

6 Vroom! Eat up!

TEC61214

Dear Parent,

We are making a **School Bus** snack soon. We would be grateful if you could help by providing the following ingredient(s):

_____

_____

_____

We need the ingredient(s) listed above by _____.

date

Please let me know if you are able to send the ingredient(s).

Thank you,

_____

teacher

- -

School Bus

☐ Yes, I am able to send the ingredient(s).

☐ No, I am unable to send the ingredient(s) this time.

_____

parent signature

The Best of The Mailbox® *Kids in the Kitchen* • ©The Mailbox® Books • TEC61214

I Made a School Bus Snack in School Today!

My favorite part was _____.

It tasted _____.

This is what it looked like:

Chef's signature: _____

The Best of The Mailbox® *Kids in the Kitchen* • ©The Mailbox® Books • TEC61214

Apple Pie Muffin

Ingredients for one:

½ English muffin
butter or margarine
apple slices (soaked in lemon juice if desired)
cinnamon-and-sugar mixture

Utensils and supplies:

empty shaker
toaster oven tray
toaster oven
plastic knife for each child
paper plate for each child

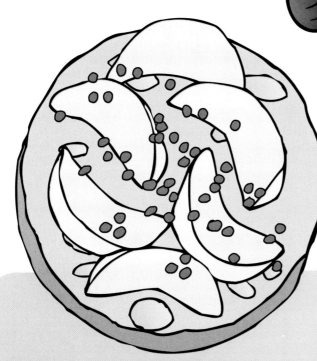

Teacher preparation:

- Arrange the supplies and ingredients for easy student access.
- Display the recipe cards from page 11. Or give each student a copy of page 10; then ask her to color and cut apart the booklet pages and staple them in order.

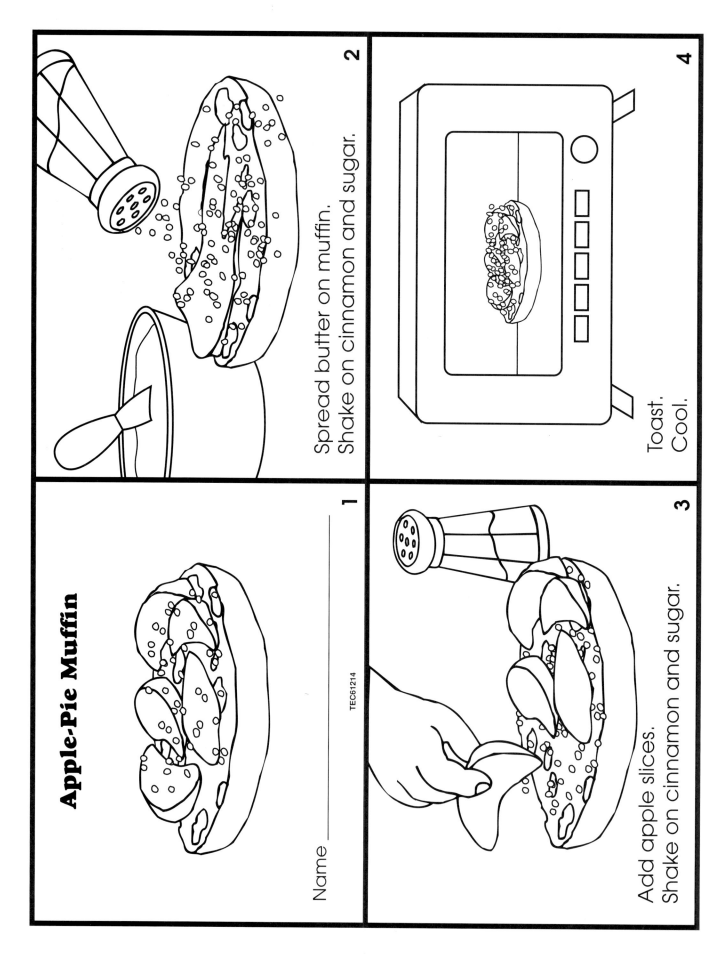

Apple-Pie Muffin

Name _____

TEC61214

1

Spread butter on muffin.
Shake on cinnamon and sugar.

2

Add apple slices.
Shake on cinnamon and sugar.

3

Toast.
Cool.

4

Apple-Pie Muffin

1

TEC61214

2

Spread butter on muffin.
Shake on cinnamon and sugar.

3

Add apple slices.
Shake on cinnamon and sugar.

4

Toast.
Cool.

Dear Parent,

We are making an **Apple-Pie Muffin** snack soon. We would be grateful if you could help by providing the following ingredient(s):

_____

_____

_____

We need the ingredient(s) listed above by _____.
date

Please let me know if you are able to send the ingredient(s).

Thank you,

_____
teacher

Apple-Pie Muffin

☐ Yes, I am able to send the ingredient(s).

☐ No, I am unable to send the ingredient(s) this time.

_____
parent signature

The Best of The Mailbox® *Kids in the Kitchen* • ©The Mailbox® Books • TEC61214

I Made an Apple-Pie Muffin in School Today!

My favorite part was _____.

It tasted _____.

This is what it looked like:

Chef's signature: _____

The Best of The Mailbox® *Kids in the Kitchen* • ©The Mailbox® Books • TEC61214

Apple Tree Treat

Ingredients for one:

1 Ritz cracker
1 graham cracker section
green-tinted frosting
4 red M&M's Minis (apples)

Utensils and supplies:

1 napkin for each child
1 plastic knife for each child

Teacher preparation:

- Arrange the supplies and ingredients for easy student access.
- Display the recipe cards from page 15. Or give each student a copy of page 14; then ask her to color and cut apart the booklet pages and staple them in order.

adapted from an idea by Julie Fallenstein-Johnson, Plymouth, MN

Apple Tree Treat

Name _____

TEC61214

1

2

Spread.

3

Spread.

4

Put together.

5

Add 4 apples.

6

Eat!

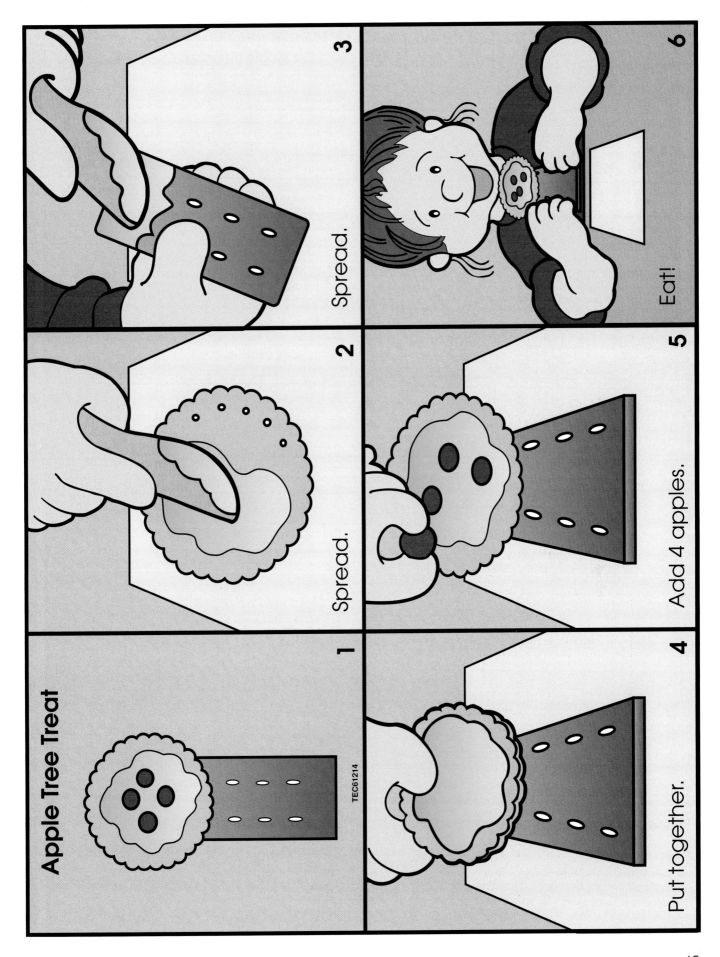

Apple Tree Treat

1

2
Spread.

3
Spread.

4
Put together.

5
Add 4 apples.

6
Eat!

TEC61214

Dear Parent,

   We are making an **Apple Tree Treat** soon. We would be grateful if you could help by providing the following ingredient(s):

_____

_____

_____

We need the ingredient(s) listed above by _____.
                                                        date

Please let me know if you are able to send the ingredient(s).
                    Thank you,

                    _____
                                    teacher

Apple Tree Treat

☐ Yes, I am able to send the ingredient(s).
☐ No, I am unable to send the ingredient(s) this time.

                    _____
                                parent signature

I Made an Apple Tree Treat in School Today!

My favorite part was _____.

It tasted _____.

This is what it looked like:

Chef's signature: _____

Firefighter's Ladder

Ingredients for one:

graham cracker (four sections)
frosting or flavored cream cheese
9 pretzel sticks

Utensils and supplies:

paper plate for each child
plastic knife for each child

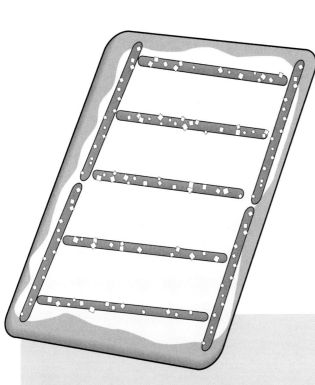

Teacher preparation:

- Arrange the supplies and ingredients for easy student access.
- Display the recipe cards from page 19. Or give each student a copy of page 18; then ask her to color and cut apart the booklet pages and staple them in order.

Jana Sanderson—PreK, Rainbow School, Stockton, CA

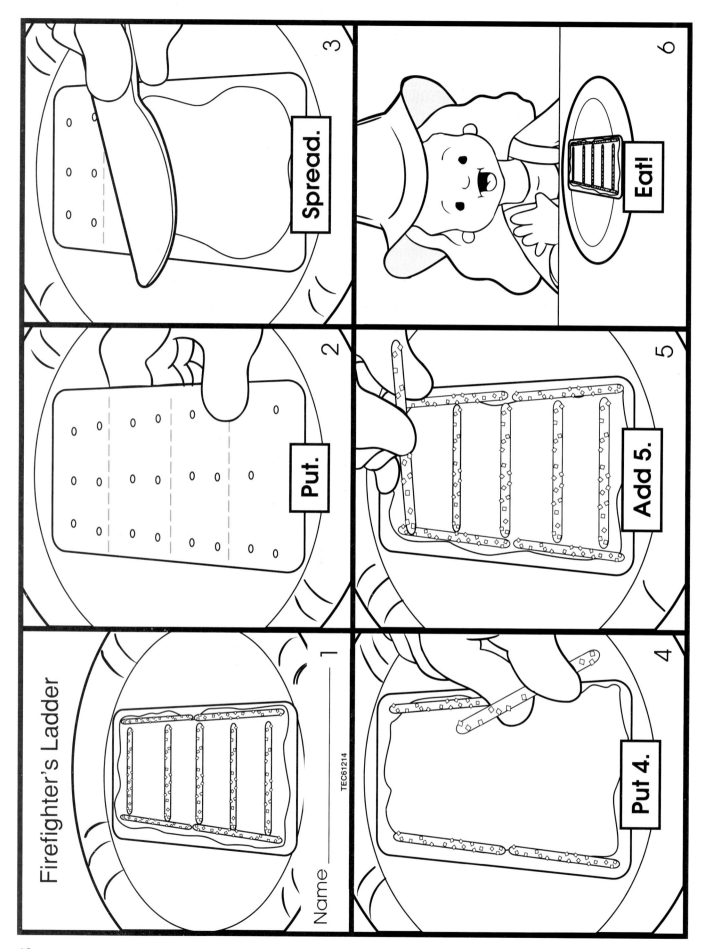

Firefighter's Ladder

Name _____

TEC61214

Put.

Spread.

Put 4.

Add 5.

Eat!

1

2

3

4

5

6

Firefighter's Ladder

TEC61214

1

Put.

2

Spread.

3

Put 4.

4

Add 5.

5

Eat!

6

Dear Parent,

We are making a **Firefighter's Ladder** snack soon. We would be grateful if you could help by providing the following ingredient(s):

_____

_____

_____

We need the ingredient(s) listed above by _____.

date

Please let me know if you are able to send the ingredient(s).

Thank you,

_____

teacher

- -

Firefighter's Ladder

☐ Yes, I am able to send the ingredient(s).

☐ No, I am unable to send the ingredient(s) this time.

_____

parent signature

I Made a Firefighter's Ladder in School Today!

My favorite part was _____.

It tasted _____.

This is what it looked like:

Chef's signature: _____

Fire-Truck Cookie

Ingredients for one:

whole graham cracker
red frosting
chocolate sandwich cookie
black decorating gel

Utensils and supplies:

napkin for each child
plastic knife for each child

Teacher preparation:

- Arrange the supplies and ingredients for easy student access.
- Display the recipe cards from page 23. Or give each student a copy of page 22; then ask her to color and cut apart the booklet pages and staple them in order.

Jeannie Coulter—Preschool Special Education • Wilton Elementary • Wilton, IA

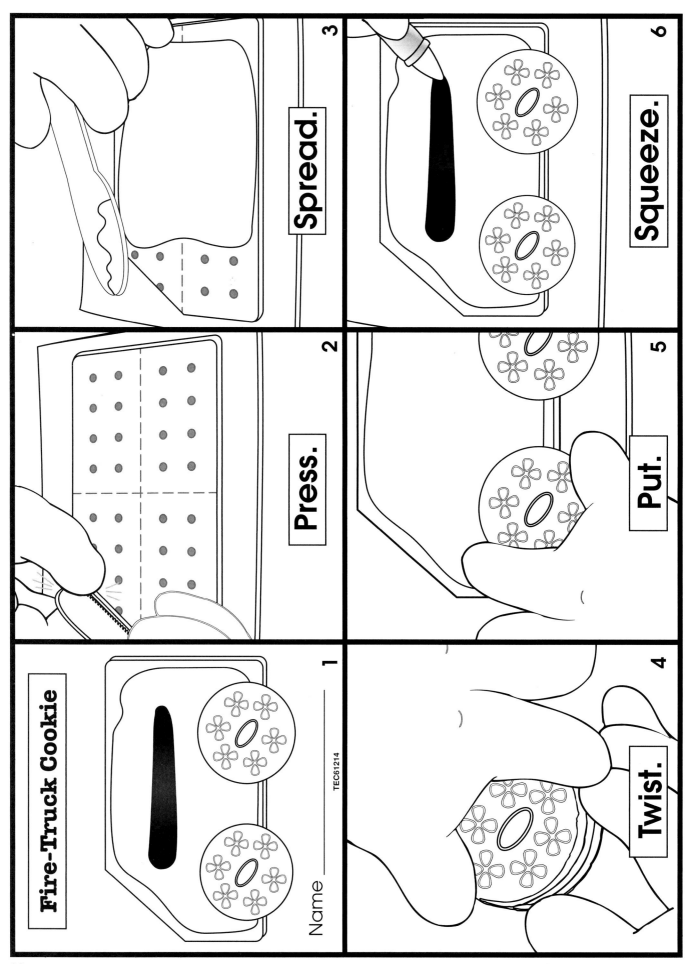

3 Spread.

6 Squeeze.

2 Press.

5 Put.

Fire-Truck Cookie

1

TEC61214

Name _____

4 Twist.

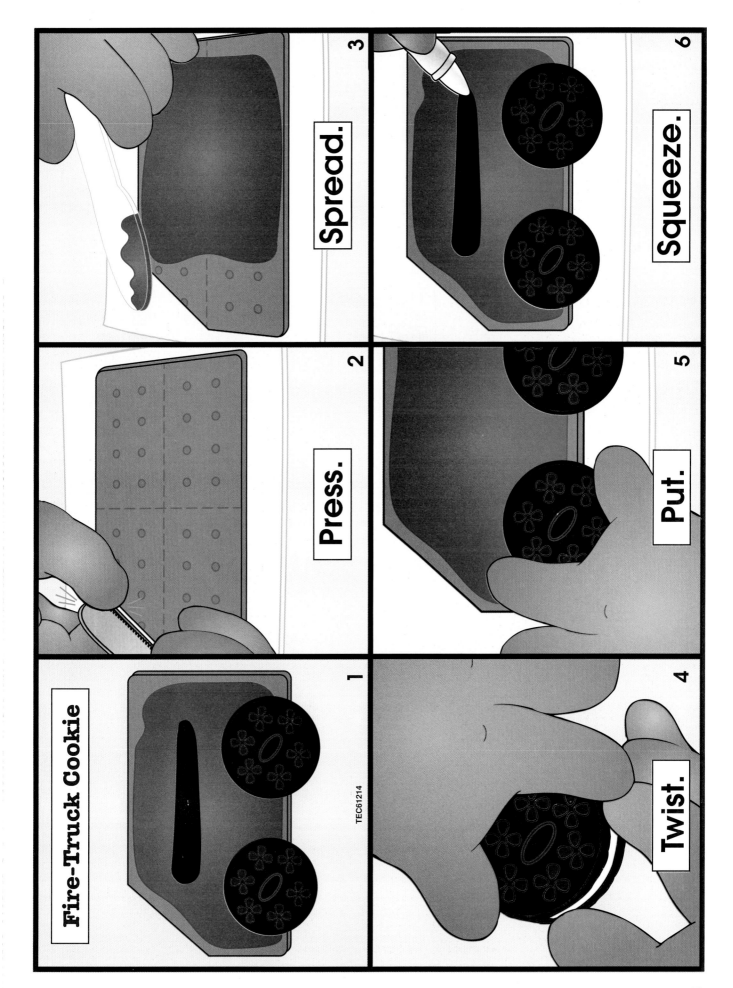

Fire-Truck Cookie

1

2 Press.

3 Spread.

4 Twist.

5 Put.

6 Squeeze.

TEC61214

Dear Parent,

 We are making a **Fire-Truck Cookie** snack soon. We would be grateful if you could help by providing the following ingredient(s):

_____

_____

_____

We need the ingredient(s) listed above by _____.
 date

Please let me know if you are able to send the ingredient(s).
 Thank you,

 _____
 teacher

Fire-Truck Cookie

☐ Yes, I am able to send the ingredient(s).
☐ No, I am unable to send the ingredient(s) this time.

 _____
 parent signature

I Made a Fire-Truck Cookie in School Today!

My favorite part was _____.

It tasted _____.

This is what it looked like:

Chef's signature: _____

Monster Mash

Ingredients for one:

package of instant oatmeal
2 mini chocolate chips
black decorating gel
2 pieces of puffed corn cereal
hot water (enough to make each bowl of oatmeal)

Utensils and supplies:

plastic bowl for each child
spoon for each child
items for heating water (such as a teakettle
    and stovetop or a microwave)

Teacher preparation:

- Arrange the supplies and ingredients for easy student access.
- Display the recipe cards from page 27. Or give each student a copy of page 26; then ask her to color and cut apart the booklet pages and staple them in order.

Jeanine Trofholz—Three-Year-Olds • St. Luke's Rainbow Preschool • Columbus, NE

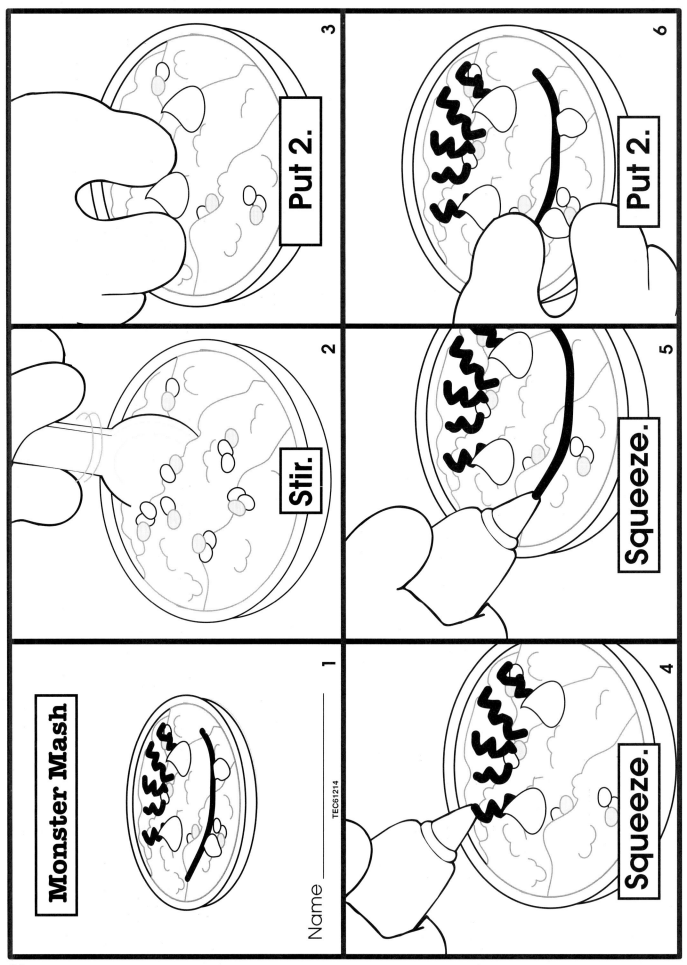

Monster Mash

1

Name _____

TEC61214

2

Stir.

3

Put 2.

4

Squeeze.

5

Squeeze.

6

Put 2.

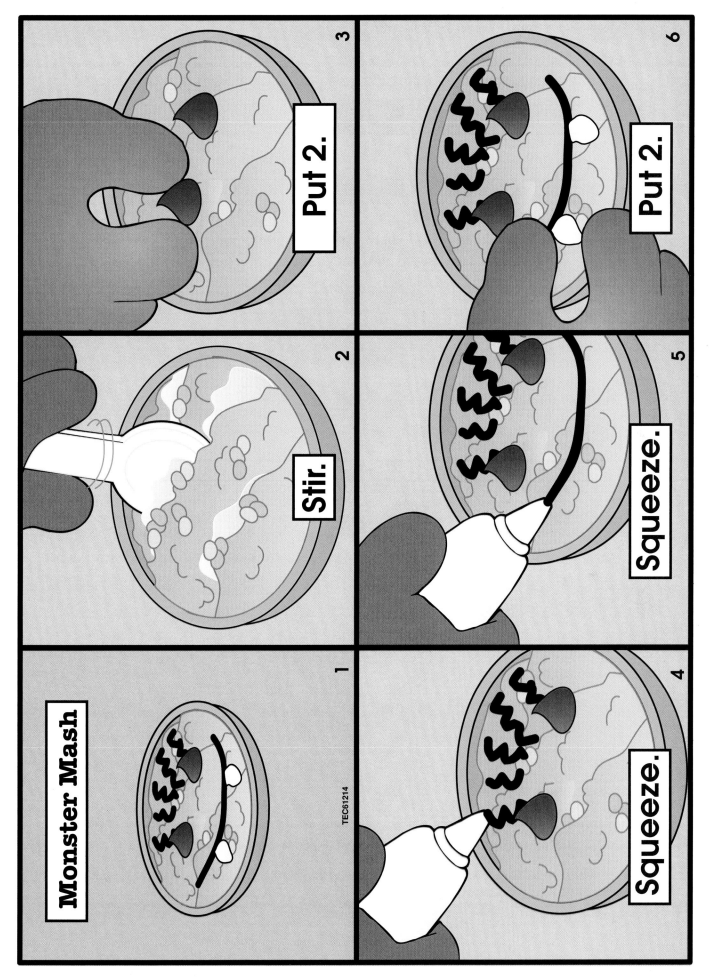

Dear Parent,

We are making a **Monster Mash** snack soon. We would be grateful if you could help by providing the following ingredient(s):

_____

_____

_____

We need the ingredient(s) listed above by _____.
date

Please let me know if you are able to send the ingredient(s).

Thank you,

_____
teacher

- -

Monster Mash

☐ Yes, I am able to send the ingredient(s).

☐ No, I am unable to send the ingredient(s) this time.

_____
parent signature

I Made Monster Mash in School Today!

My favorite part was _____.

It tasted _____.

This is what it looked like:

Chef's signature: _____

Jack-o'-Lantern Cookie

Ingredients for one:

slice of refrigerated sugar-cookie dough
orange decorator sugar
7 mini chocolate chips

Utensils and supplies:

plastic knife for each child
napkin for each child
aluminum foil
permanent marker

baking sheet
oven
oven mitt
spatula

Teacher preparation:

- Freeze the dough for 30 minutes. Personalize a foil square for each child.
- Arrange the supplies and ingredients for easy student access.
- Display the recipe cards from page 31. Or give each student a copy of page 30; then ask her to color and cut apart the booklet pages and staple them in order.

Desiree Magnani and Toni-Ann Maisano—Preschool • Babes in Toyland, Staten Island, NY

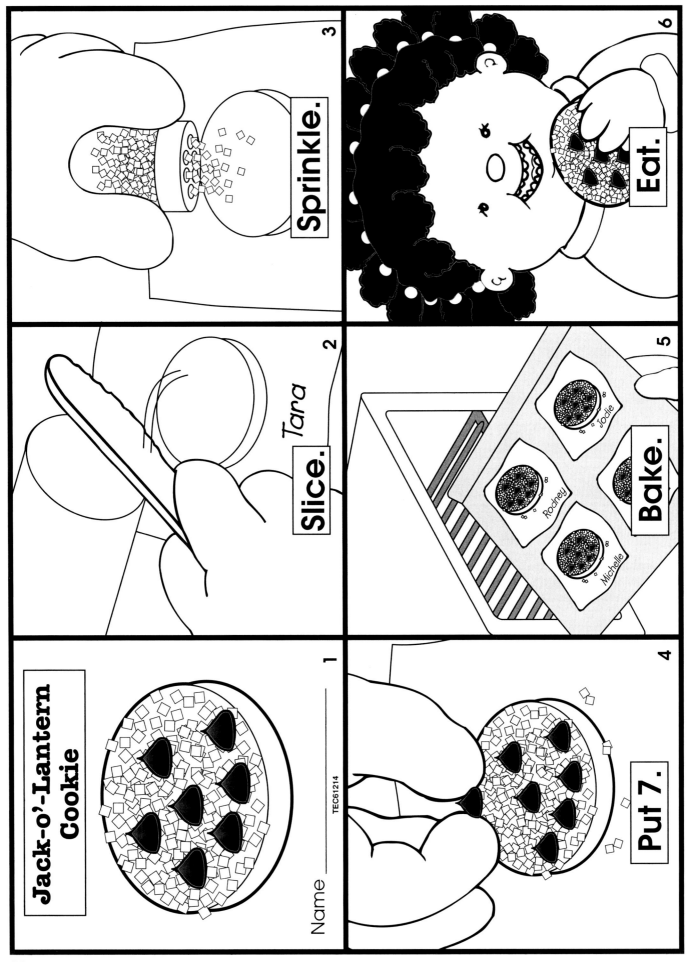

3

Sprinkle.

6

Eat.

2

Slice.

Tara

5

Bake.

Jodie

Rodney

Michelle

1

Jack-o'-Lantern
Cookie

Name _____

TEC61214

4

Put 7.

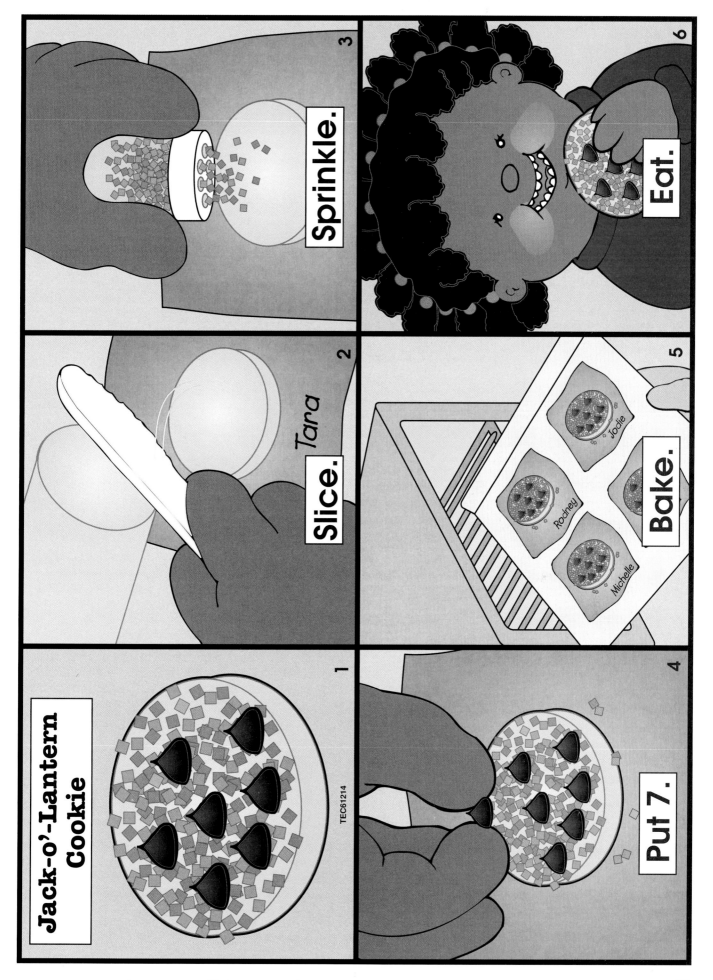

Dear Parent,

We are making **Jack-o'-Lantern Cookies** soon. We would be grateful if you could help by providing the following ingredient(s):

_____

_____

_____

We need the ingredient(s) listed above by _____.

                                                                    date

Please let me know if you are able to send the ingredient(s).

                     Thank you,

                                _____

                                       teacher

- -

Jack-o'-Lantern Cookies

☐ Yes, I am able to send the ingredient(s).

☐ No, I am unable to send the ingredient(s) this time.

                                _____

                                 parent signature

I Made a Jack-o'-Lantern Cookie in School Today!

My favorite part was _____.

It tasted _____.

This is what it looked like:

Chef's signature: _____

Frozen Pumpkin Square

Ingredients for one:

two square graham crackers
1 tsp. pumpkin-pie filling
3 tbsp. whipped topping

Utensils and supplies:

measuring spoons:
    tablespoon, teaspoon
disposable bowl for each child
plastic spoon for each child
freezer

Teacher preparation:

- Arrange the supplies and ingredients for easy student access.
- Display the recipe cards from page 35. Or give each student a copy
  of page 34; then ask her to color and cut apart the booklet pages and
  staple them in order.

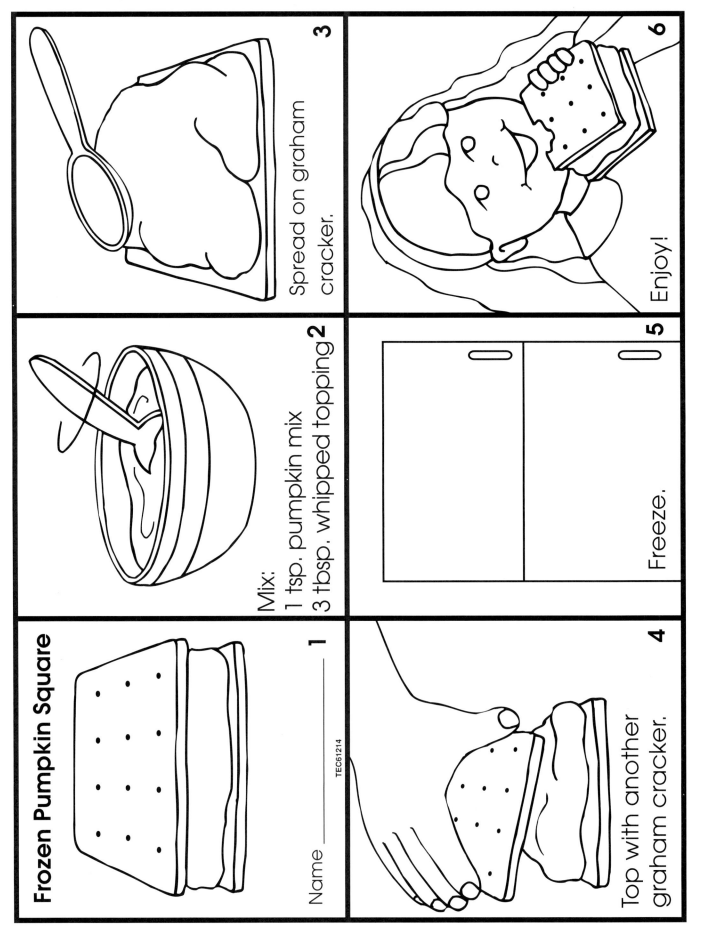

Frozen Pumpkin Square

Name _____

TEC61214

1

2

Mix:
1 tsp. pumpkin mix
3 tbsp. whipped topping

3

Spread on graham cracker.

4

Top with another graham cracker.

5

Freeze.

6

Enjoy!

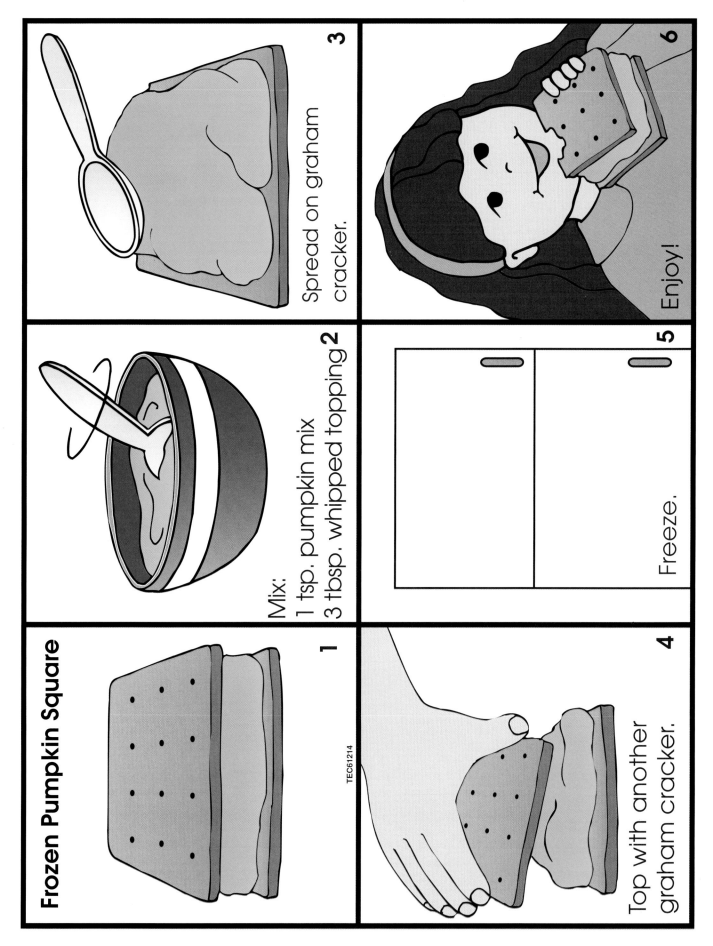

Frozen Pumpkin Square

1

2

Mix:
1 tsp. pumpkin mix
3 tbsp. whipped topping

3

Spread on graham cracker.

4

Top with another graham cracker.

5

Freeze.

6

Enjoy!

TEC61214

Dear Parent,

We are making **Frozen Pumpkin Squares** soon. We would be grateful if you could help by providing the following ingredient(s):

_____

_____

_____

We need the ingredient(s) listed above by _____.
                                                    date

Please let me know if you are able to send the ingredient(s).

Thank you,

_____
                teacher

Frozen Pumpkin Squares

☐ Yes, I am able to send the ingredient(s).

☐ No, I am unable to send the ingredient(s) this time.

_____
            parent signature

I Made a Frozen Pumpkin Square in School Today!

My favorite part was _____.

It tasted _____.

This is what it looked like:

Chef's signature: _____

Tasty Turkey Roll-Up

Ingredients for one:

flour tortilla
whipped cream cheese
2 slices of turkey sandwich meat
cranberry sauce

Utensils and supplies:

plastic knife for each child
paper plate for each child
spoon for each child

Teacher preparation:

- Arrange the supplies and ingredients for easy student access.
- Display the recipe cards from page 39. Or give each student a copy of page 38; then ask her to color and cut apart the booklet pages and staple them in order.

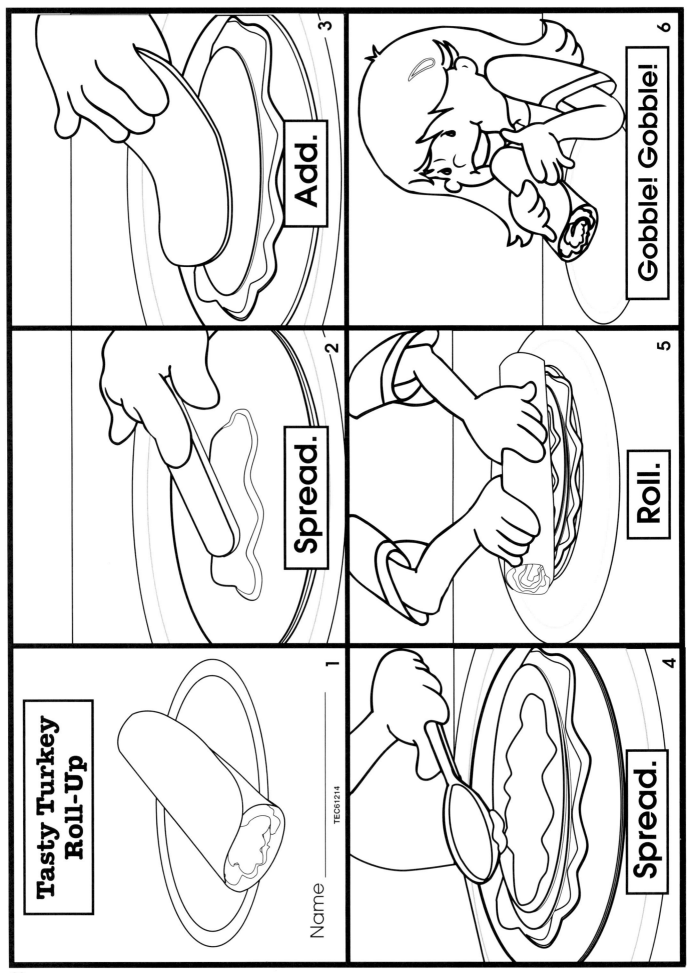

3   **Add.**

6   **Gobble! Gobble!**

2   **Spread.**

5   **Roll.**

Tasty Turkey Roll-Up   1

Name _____

TEC61214

4   **Spread.**

The Best of The Mailbox® *Kids in the Kitchen* • ©The Mailbox® Books • TEC61214

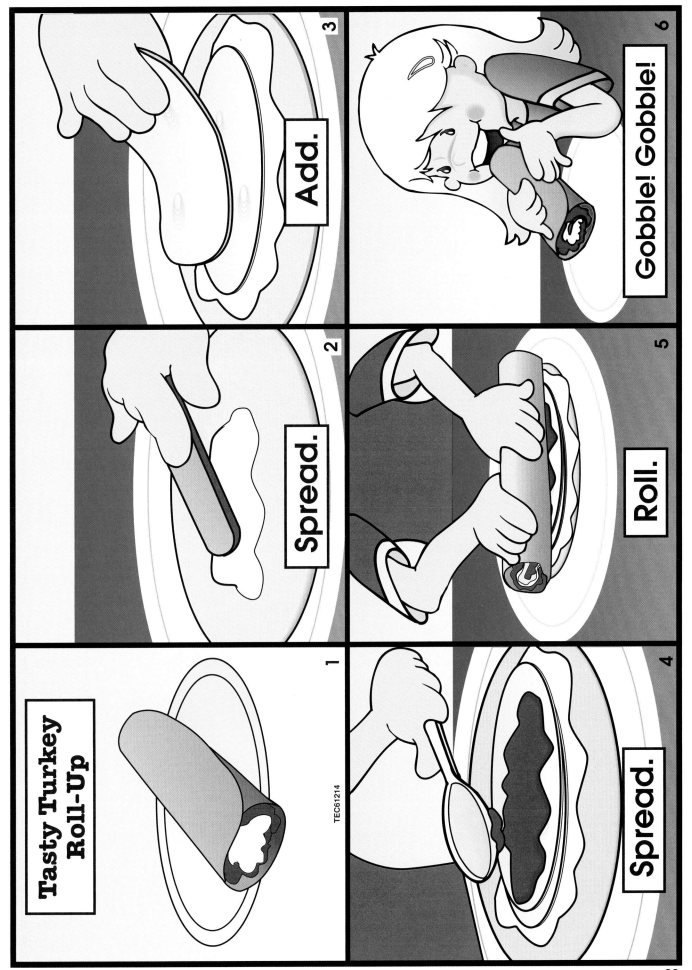

Dear Parent,

We are making a **Tasty Turkey Roll-Up** snack soon. We would be grateful if you could help by providing the following ingredient(s):

_____

_____

_____

We need the ingredient(s) listed above by _____.
date

Please let me know if you are able to send the ingredient(s).

Thank you,

_____
teacher

- -

Tasty Turkey Roll-Up

☐ Yes, I am able to send the ingredient(s).
☐ No, I am unable to send the ingredient(s) this time.

_____
parent signature

I Made a Tasty Turkey Roll-Up in School Today!

My favorite part was _____.

It tasted _____.

This is what it looked like:

Chef's signature: _____

Reindeer Pop

Ingredients for one:

banana half
3 M&M's Minis candies
2 mini pretzels

melted semisweet baking chocolate
chocolate frosting

Utensils and supplies:

piece of waxed paper for each child
craft stick for each child

Teacher Preparation:

- Arrange the supplies and ingredients for easy student access.
- Display the recipe cards from page 43. Or give each student a copy of page 42; then ask her to color and cut apart the booklet pages and staple them in order.

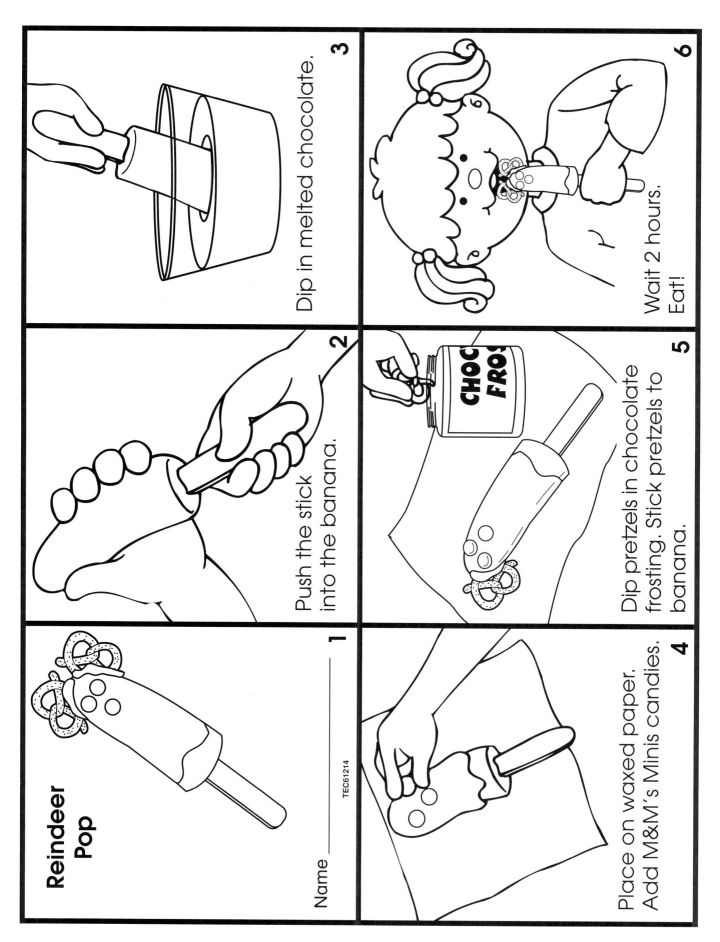

3 Dip in melted chocolate.

6 Wait 2 hours. Eat!

2 Push the stick into the banana.

5 Dip pretzels in chocolate frosting. Stick pretzels to banana.

Reindeer Pop

1

TEC61214

Name _____

4 Place on waxed paper. Add M&M's Minis candies.

CHOC FROS

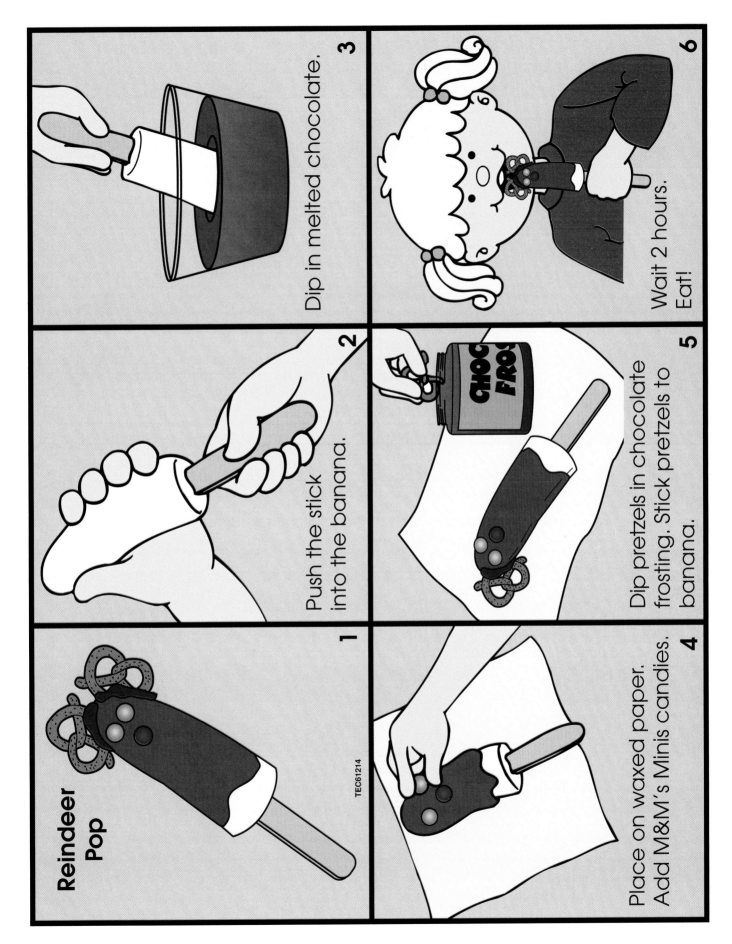

Reindeer Pop

1

2

Push the stick into the banana.

3

Dip in melted chocolate.

4

Place on waxed paper. Add M&M's Minis candies.

5

Dip pretzels in chocolate frosting. Stick pretzels to banana.

6

Wait 2 hours. Eat!

TEC61214

Dear Parent,
   We are making **Reindeer Pops** soon. We would be grateful if you could help by
providing the following ingredient(s):

_____

_____

_____

We need the ingredient(s) listed above by _____.
                                                                    date

Please let me know if you are able to send the ingredient(s).
                        Thank you,

                        _____
                                    teacher

- -

Reindeer Pop

☐ Yes, I am able to send the ingredient(s).
☐ No, I am unable to send the ingredient(s) this time.

                        _____
                                  parent signature

I Made a Reindeer Pop in School Today!

My favorite part was _____.

It tasted _____.

This is what it looked like:

Chef's signature: _____

A Wreath You Eat!

Ingredients for one:

mini bagel half
green-tinted whipped cream cheese
M&M's Minis candies

Utensils and supplies:

napkin for each child
plastic knife for each child

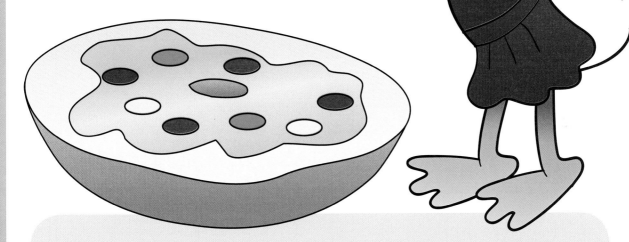

Teacher preparation:

- Arrange the supplies and ingredients for easy student access.
- Display the recipe cards from page 47. Or give each student a copy of page 46; then ask her to color and cut apart the booklet pages and staple them in order.

Julie Witherell, Maywood School, Monona, WI

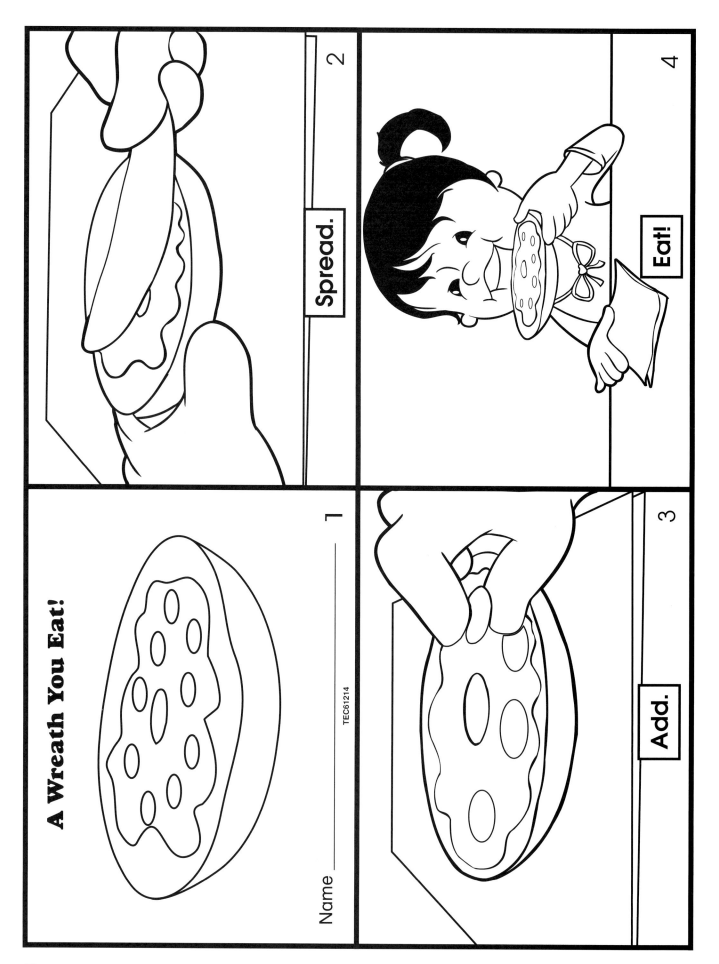

A Wreath You Eat!

1

Name _____

TEC61214

Spread.

2

Add.

3

Eat!

4

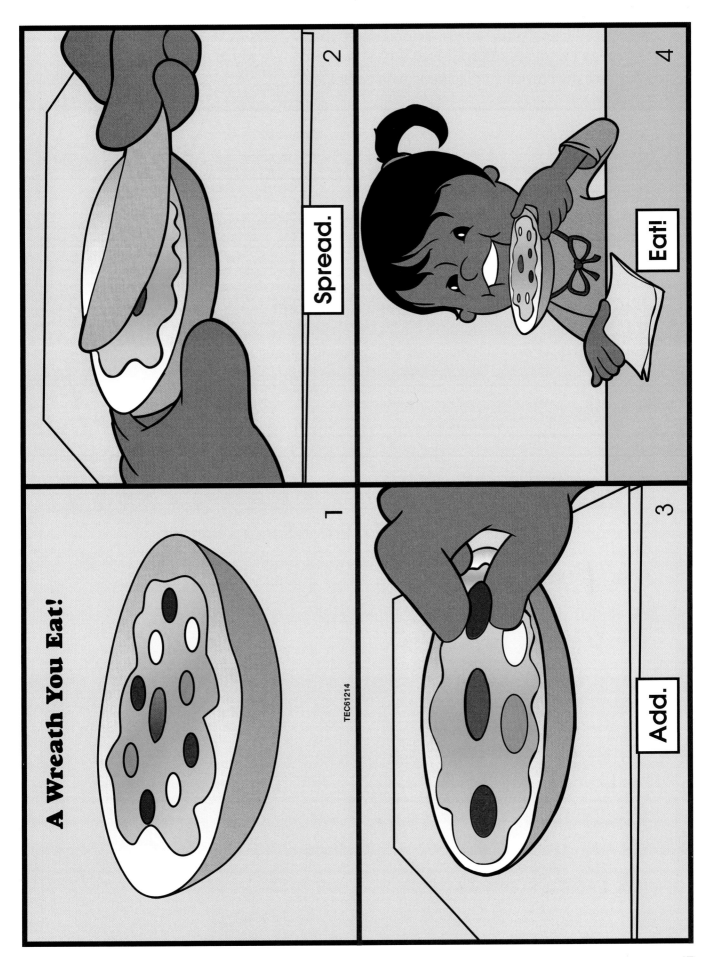

Dear Parent,

We are making **A Wreath You Eat** snack soon. We would be grateful if you could help by providing the following ingredient(s):

_____

_____

_____

We need the ingredient(s) listed above by _____.
 date

Please let me know if you are able to send the ingredient(s).

Thank you,

_____
teacher

- -

A Wreath You Eat!

☐ Yes, I am able to send the ingredient(s).

☐ No, I am unable to send the ingredient(s) this time.

_____
parent signature

I Made A Wreath You Eat in School Today!

My favorite part was _____.

It tasted _____.

This is what it looked like:

Chef's signature: _____

Santa Mix

Ingredients for one:

M&M's Minis candies (elf noses)
small pretzels (reindeer antlers)
Kix cereal (Santa's buttons)
O-shaped cereal (reindeer food)

Utensils and supplies:

bowl for each ingredient
tablespoon for each ingredient
paper cup for each child

Teacher preparation:

- Arrange the supplies and ingredients for easy student access.
- Display the recipe cards from page 51. Or give each student a copy of page 50; then ask her to color and cut apart the booklet pages and staple them in order.

Anne Arceneaux, Ward School, Jennings, LA

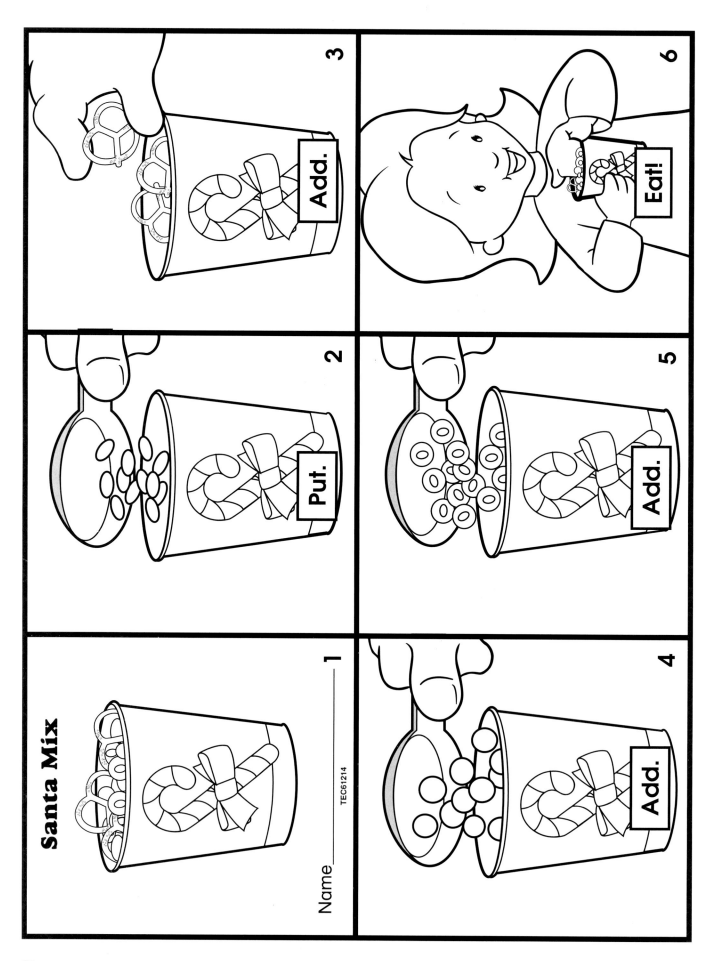

Santa Mix

Name _____

TEC61214

1

Put.

2

Add.

3

Add.

4

Add.

5

Eat!

6

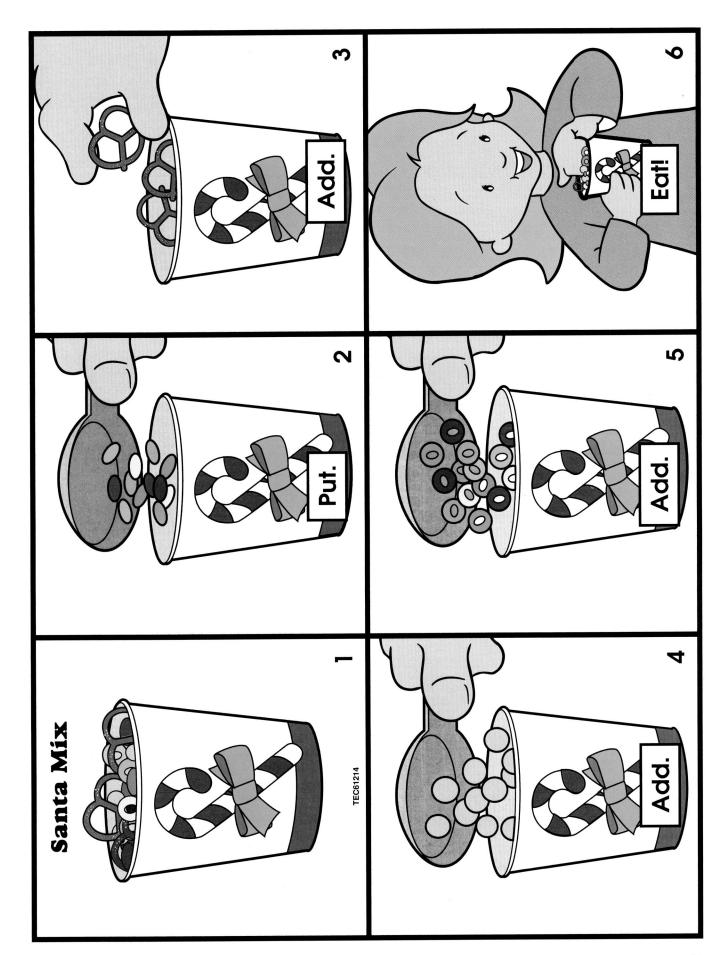

Dear Parent,
   We are making a **Santa Mix** snack soon. We would be grateful if you could help by providing the following ingredient(s):

_____

_____

_____

We need the ingredient(s) listed above by _____.
                                                                    date

Please let me know if you are able to send the ingredient(s).
                         Thank you,

                    _____
                                   teacher

— —

Santa Mix

☐ Yes, I am able to send the ingredient(s).
☐ No, I am unable to send the ingredient(s) this time.

                    _____
                            parent signature

I Made Santa Mix in School Today!

My favorite part was _____.

It tasted _____.

This is what it looked like:

Chef's signature: _____

Snowfolk Face

Ingredients for one:

rice cake
soft cream cheese
7 mini chocolate chips
cheese triangle

Utensils And Supplies:

plastic knife for each child
napkin for each child

Teacher Preparation:

- Arrange the supplies and ingredients for easy student access.
- Display the recipe cards from page 55. Or give each student a copy of page 54; then ask her to color and cut apart the booklet pages and staple them in order.

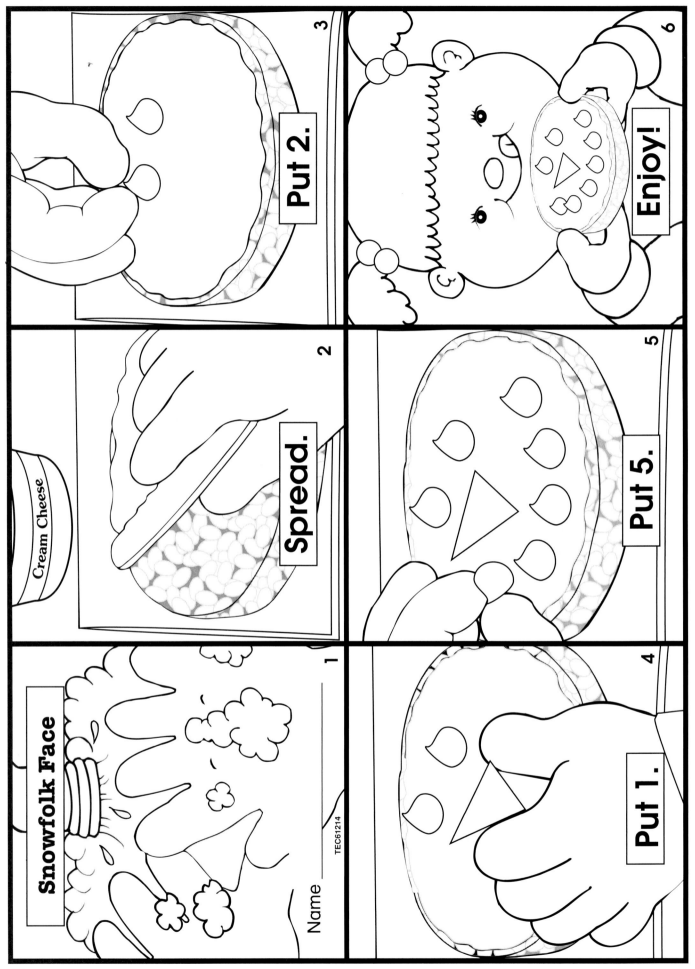

Snowfolk Face

1

Name _____

TEC61214

Spread.

2

Cream Cheese

Put 2.

3

Put 1.

4

Put 5.

5

Enjoy!

6

Dear Parent,

   We are making a **Snowfolk Face** snack soon. We would be grateful if you could help by providing the following ingredient(s):

_____

_____

_____

We need the ingredient(s) listed above by _____.
date

Please let me know if you are able to send the ingredient(s).

Thank you,

_____
teacher

Snowfolk Face

☐ Yes, I am able to send the ingredient(s).
☐ No, I am unable to send the ingredient(s) this time.

_____
parent signature

I Made a Snowfolk Face in School Today!

My favorite part was _____.

It tasted _____.

This is what it looked like:

Chef's signature: _____

Snowshoe Hare

Ingredients for one:

2 round crackers
soft cream cheese
2 thin apple slices
3 M&M's Minis candies
6 shoestring potato pieces

Utensils and supplies:

paper plate for each child
plastic knife for each child

Teacher preparation:

- Arrange the supplies and ingredients for easy student access.
- Display the recipe cards from page 59. Or give each student a copy of page 58; then ask him to color and cut apart the booklet pages and staple them in order.

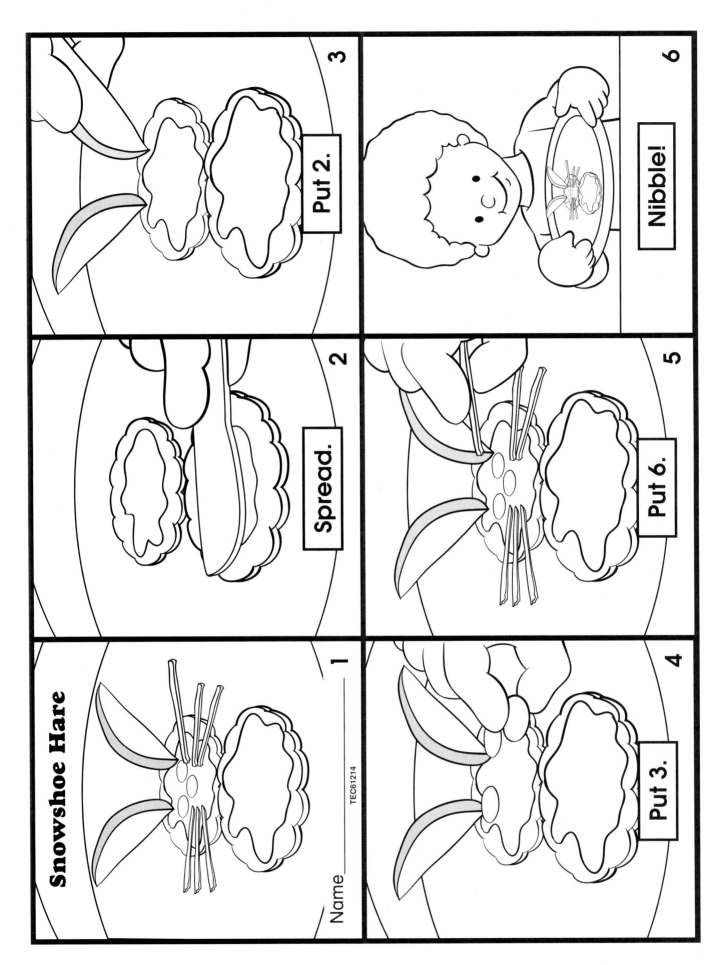

Snowshoe Hare

1

Name _____

TEC61214

2

Spread.

3

Put 2.

4

Put 3.

5

Put 6.

6

Nibble!

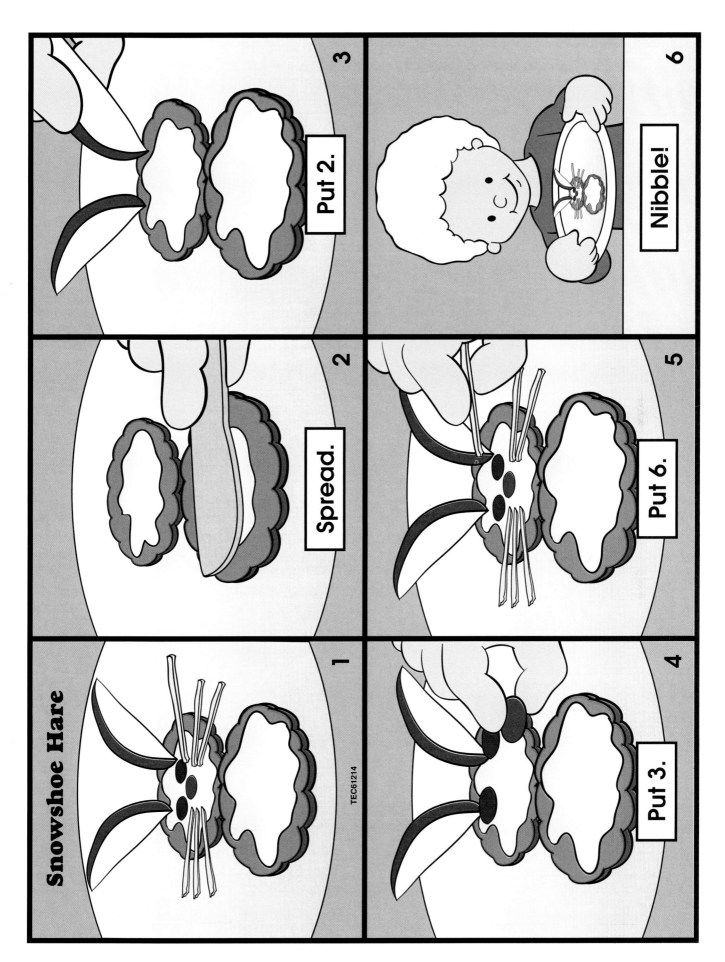

Snowshoe Hare

1

TEC61214

2

Spread.

3

Put 2.

4

Put 3.

5

Put 6.

6

Nibble!

Dear Parent,
    We are making a **Snowshoe Hare** snack soon. We would be grateful if you could help by providing the following ingredient(s):

_____

_____

_____

We need the ingredient(s) listed above by _____.
                                                        date

Please let me know if you are able to send the ingredient(s).
                        Thank you,

                        _____
                                        teacher

- -

Snowshoe Hare

☐ Yes, I am able to send the ingredient(s).
☐ No, I am unable to send the ingredient(s) this time.

                        _____
                                        parent signature

I Made a Snowshoe Hare in School Today!

My favorite part was _____.

It tasted _____.

This is what it looked like:

Chef's signature: _____

A Warm Snowflake

Ingredients for one:

8" flour tortilla
melted butter
powdered sugar (snow)

Utensils and supplies:

paper plate for each child
clean school scissors
shaker for powdered sugar
pastry brush

Teacher preparation:

- Wrap tortillas in damp paper towels and microwave for 15 to 30 seconds.
- Arrange the supplies and ingredients for easy student access.
- Display the recipe cards from page 63. Or give each student a copy of page 62; then ask him to color and cut apart the booklet pages and staple them in order.

Allison Pratt, Onalaska Kindergarten Center, Onalaska, WI

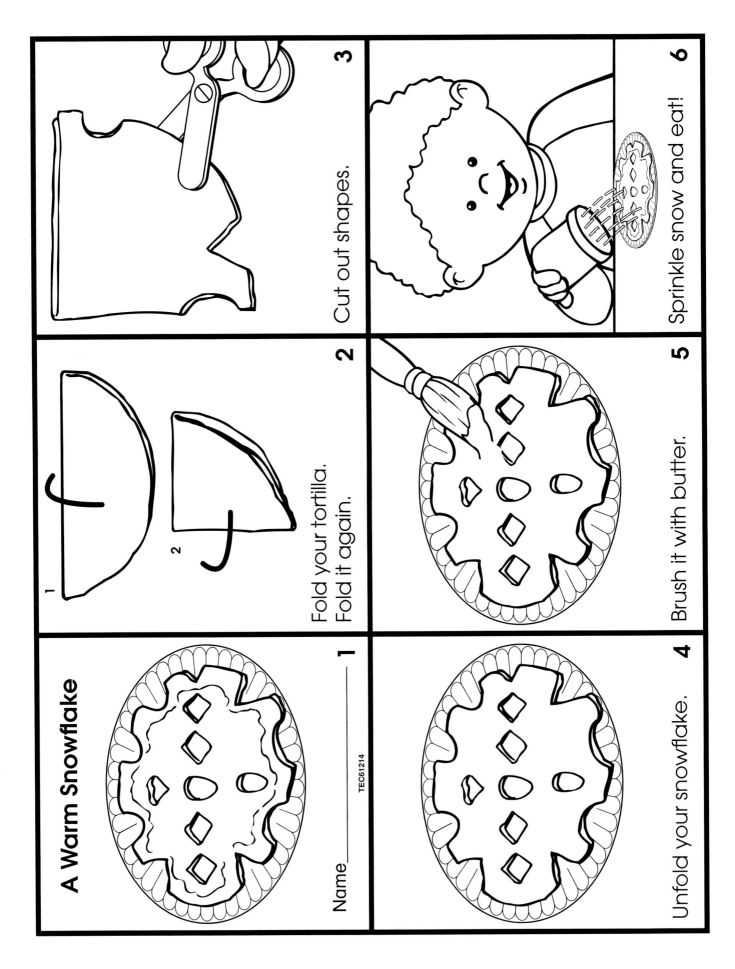

A Warm Snowflake

1

Name _____

TEC61214

2

1

2

Fold your tortilla.
Fold it again.

3

Cut out shapes.

4

Unfold your snowflake.

5

Brush it with butter.

6

Sprinkle snow and eat!

A Warm Snowflake

1

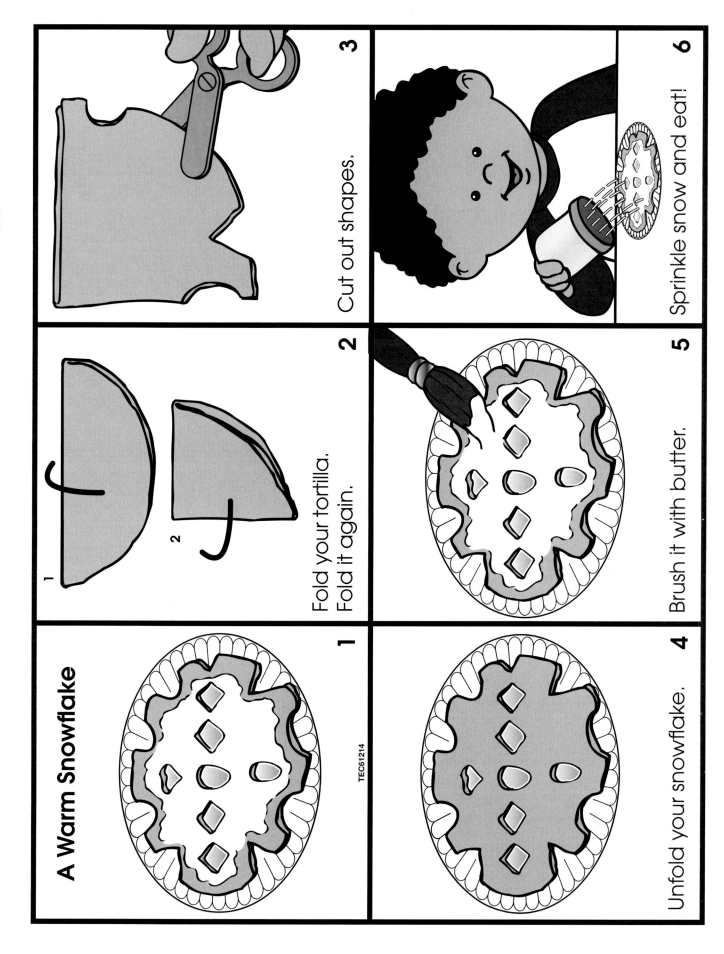

2

Fold your tortilla.
Fold it again.

3

Cut out shapes.

4

Unfold your snowflake.

5

Brush it with butter.

6

Sprinkle snow and eat!

TEC61214

Dear Parent,
  We are making a **Warm Snowflake** snack soon. We would be grateful if you could help by providing the following ingredient(s):

_____

_____

_____

We need the ingredient(s) listed above by _____.
                                                    date

Please let me know if you are able to send the ingredient(s).
                        Thank you,

                        _____
                                        teacher

- -

Warm Snowflake

☐ Yes, I am able to send the ingredient(s).
☐ No, I am unable to send the ingredient(s) this time.

                        _____
                                parent signature

I Made a Warm Snowflake in School Today!

My favorite part was _____.

It tasted _____.

This is what it looked like:

Chef's signature: _____

Ingredients for one:

banana half
3 mini chocolate chips (eyes and nose)
2 almond slices (ears)

Utensils and supplies:

3 oz. Dixie cup for each child (garden scene on the side optional)

Teacher preparation:

- Arrange the supplies and ingredients for easy student access.
- Display the recipe cards from page 67. Or give each student a copy of page 66; then ask her to color and cut apart the booklet pages and staple them in order.

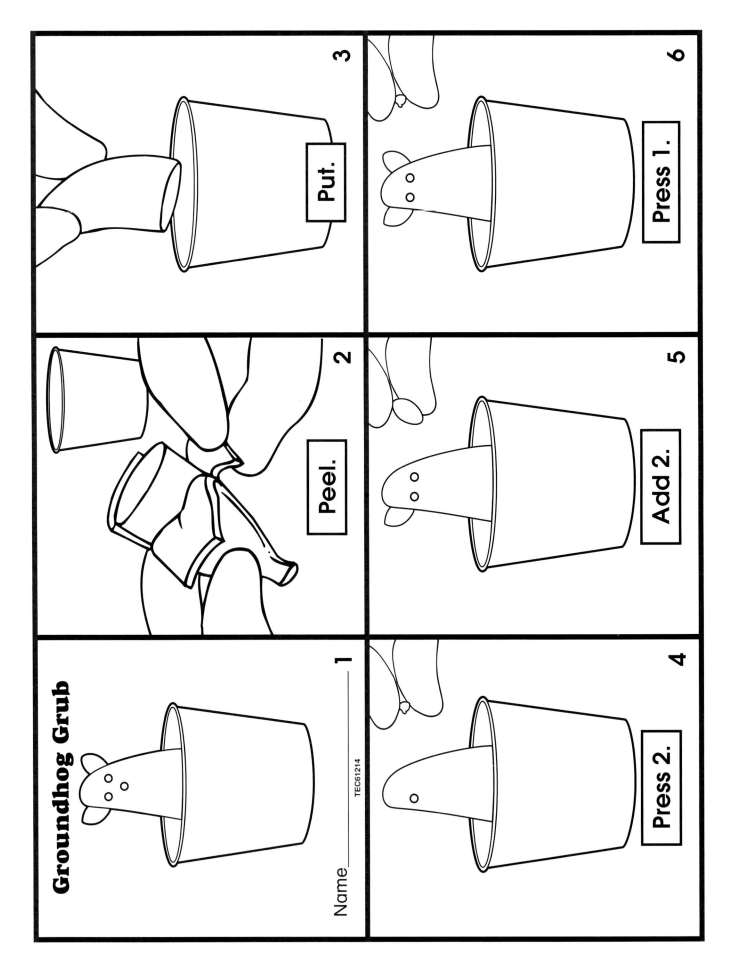

3 Put.

6 Press 1.

2 Peel.

5 Add 2.

Groundhog Grub

1

TEC61214

Name

4 Press 2.

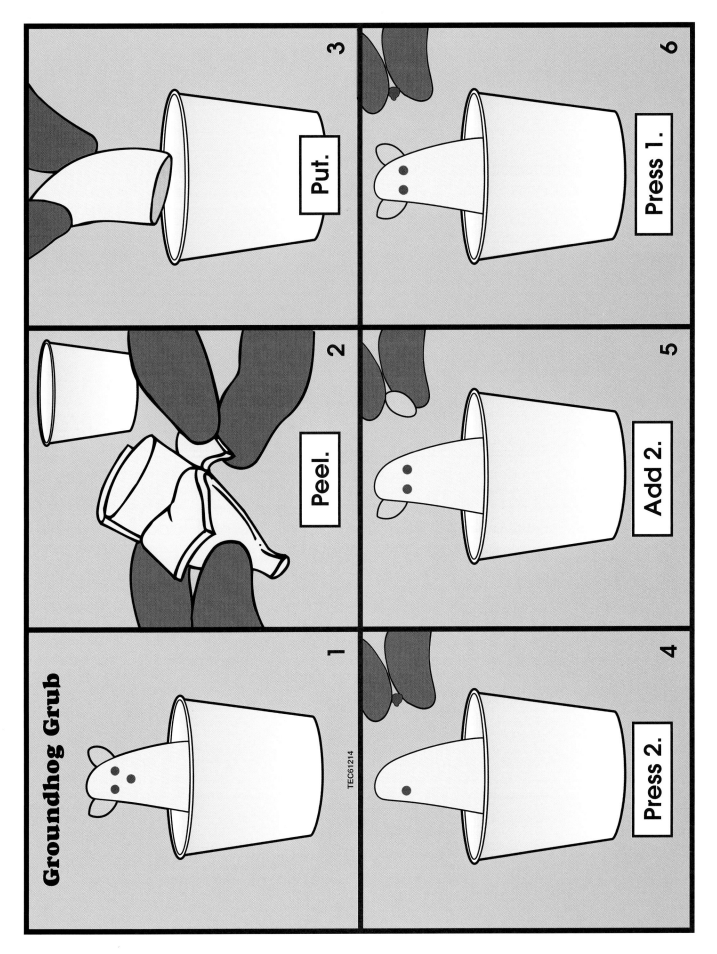

Dear Parent,

   We are making a **Groundhog Grub** snack soon. We would be grateful if you could help by providing the following ingredient(s):

_____

_____

_____

We need the ingredient(s) listed above by _____.
                                                              date

Please let me know if you are able to send the ingredient(s).

                        Thank you,

                  _____
                                teacher

- -

Groundhog Grub

☐ Yes, I am able to send the ingredient(s).

☐ No, I am unable to send the ingredient(s) this time.

                  _____
                            parent signature

I Made a Groundhog Grub Snack in School Today!

My favorite part was _____.

It tasted _____.

This is what it looked like:

Chef's signature: _____

Mouse Sandwich

Ingredients for one:

1 slice of bread
strawberry jam
1 mini chocolate chip
1 pretzel stick

Utensils and supplies:

heart-shaped cookie cutter
plastic knife for each child
napkin for each child

Teacher preparation:

- Arrange the supplies and ingredients for easy student access.
- Display the recipe cards from page 71. Or give each student a copy of page 70; then ask her to color and cut apart the booklet pages and staple them in order.

Susan Horn—St. Louis, MO

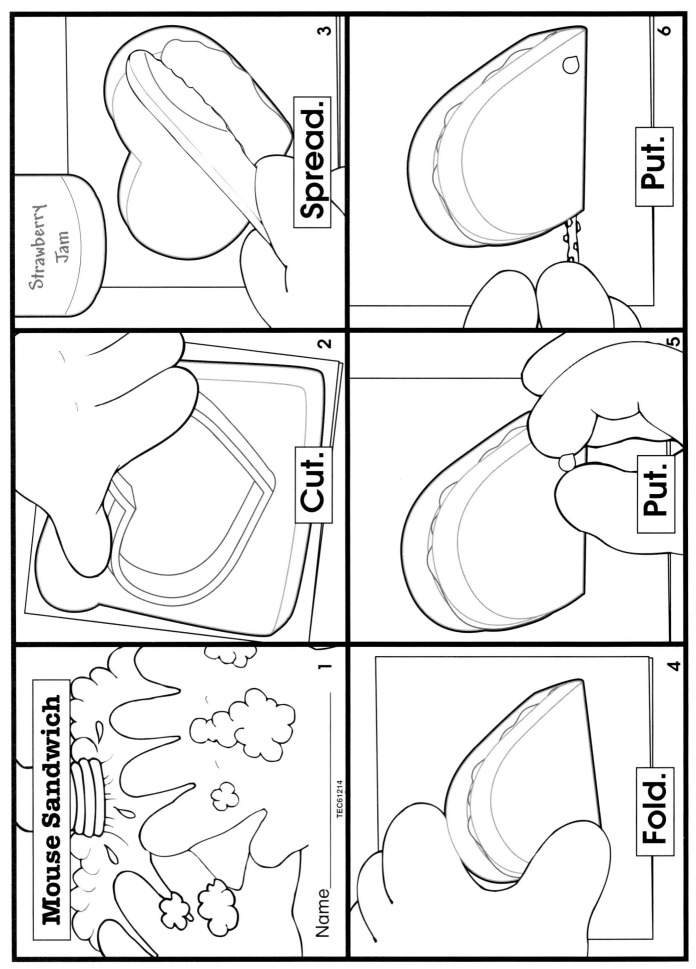

Mouse Sandwich

Name

Strawberry Jam

Spread.

Cut.

Put.

Fold.

Put.

1

2

3

4

5

6

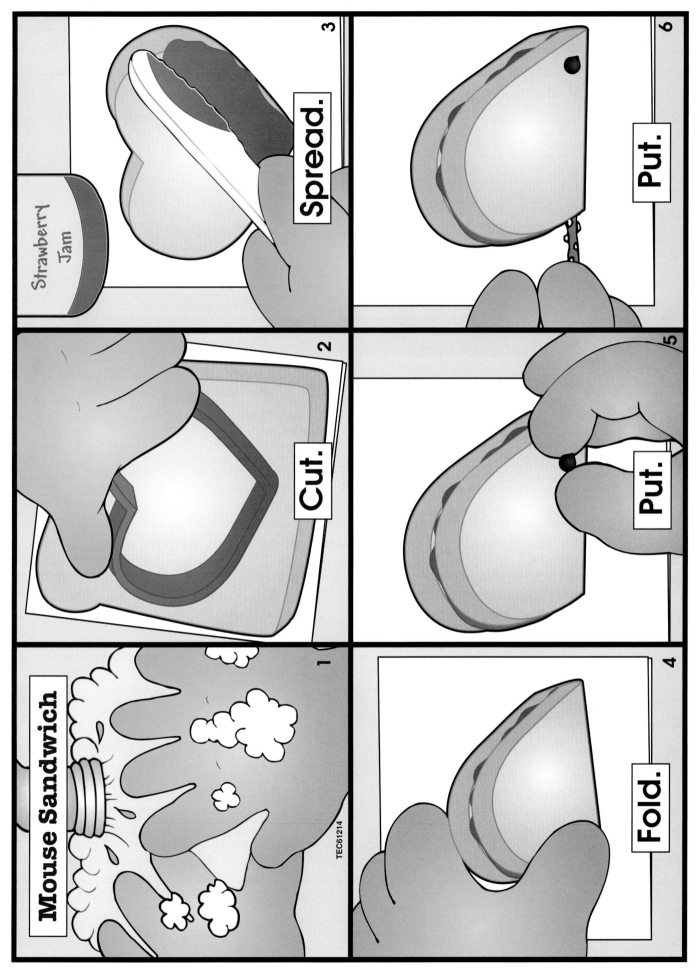

Dear Parent,

We are making a **Mouse Sandwich** snack soon. We would be grateful if you could help by providing the following ingredient(s):

_____

_____

_____

We need the ingredient(s) listed above by _____.
                                                                        date

Please let me know if you are able to send the ingredient(s).

Thank you,

_____
                        teacher

Mouse Sandwich

☐ Yes, I am able to send the ingredient(s).

☐ No, I am unable to send the ingredient(s) this time.

_____
                        parent signature

I Made a Mouse Sandwich in School Today!

My favorite part was _____.

It tasted _____.

This is what it looked like:

Chef's signature: _____

Lovebug Cookie

Ingredients for one:

large sugar cookie
strawberry-flavored frosting
2 pretzel sticks (antennae)
red decorating gel (mouth)
2 M&M's Minis candies (eyes)
mini chocolate chip (nose)

Utensils and supplies:

paper plate for each child
plastic knife for each child
2 doily quarters (wings) for each child

Teacher preparation:

• Arrange the supplies and ingredients for easy student access.
• Display the recipe cards from page 75. Or give each student a copy of page 74; then ask her to color and cut apart the booklet pages and staple them in order.

Peggy Stratton, Okeechobee, FL

Lovebug Cookie

1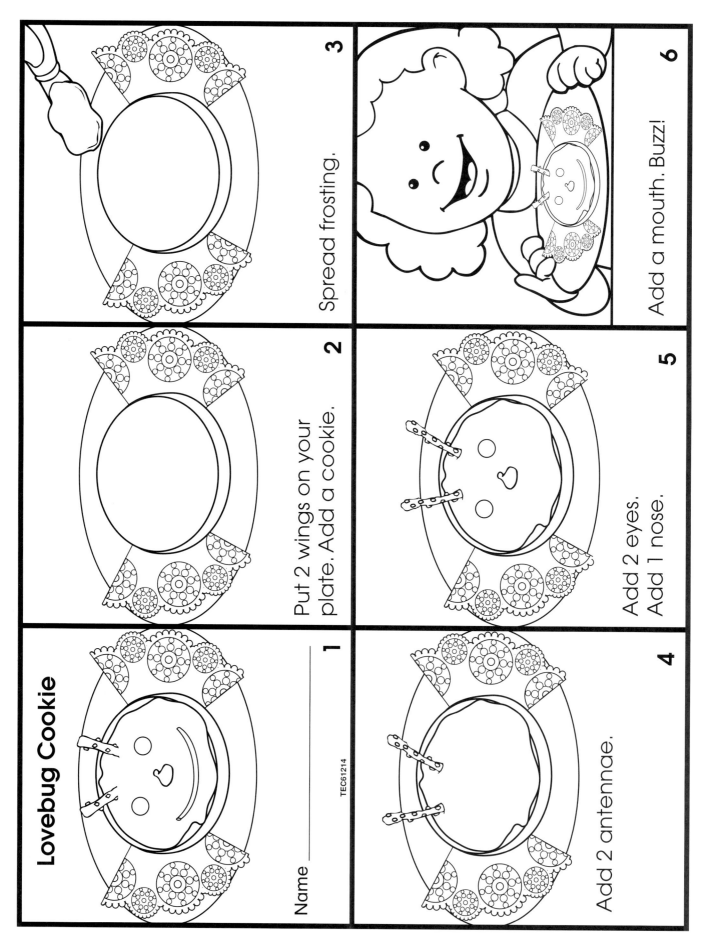

Name _____

TEC61214

2

Put 2 wings on your plate. Add a cookie.

3

Spread frosting.

4

Add 2 antennae.

5

Add 2 eyes.
Add 1 nose.

6

Add a mouth. Buzz!

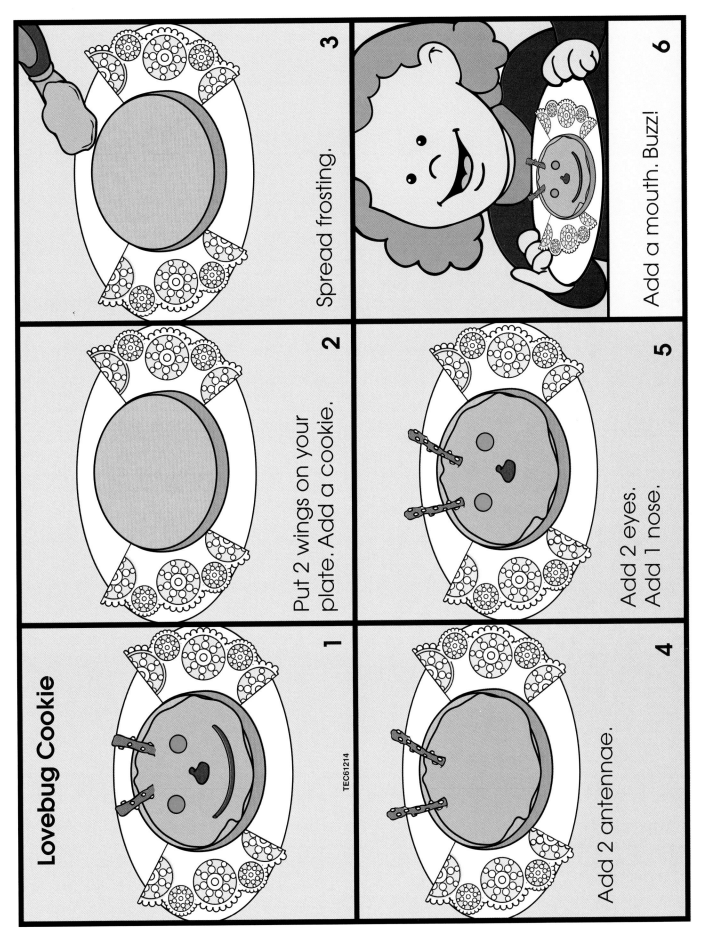

Lovebug Cookie

1

TEC61214

2

Put 2 wings on your plate. Add a cookie.

3

Spread frosting.

4

Add 2 antennae.

5

Add 2 eyes.
Add 1 nose.

6

Add a mouth. Buzz!

Dear Parent,

We are making a **Lovebug Cookie** snack soon. We would be grateful if you could help by providing the following ingredient(s):

_____

_____

_____

We need the ingredient(s) listed above by _____.
                                                                    date

Please let me know if you are able to send the ingredient(s).

Thank you,

_____
                     teacher

- -

Lovebug Cookie

☐ Yes, I am able to send the ingredient(s).

☐ No, I am unable to send the ingredient(s) this time.

_____
                parent signature

I Made a Lovebug Cookie in School Today!

My favorite part was _____.

It tasted _____.

This is what it looked like:

Chef's signature: _____

Cherry Delight

Ingredients for one:

graham cracker square
$\frac{1}{3}$ c. prepared vanilla pudding
2 spoonfuls cherry pie filling
spoonful whipped topping

Utensils and supplies:

resealable plastic sandwich bag
   for each student
rolling pin
9 oz. clear plastic cup for each student
$\frac{1}{3}$-cup measuring cup
2 serving spoons
plastic spoon for each student

Teacher preparation:

- Arrange the supplies and ingredients for easy student access.
- Display the recipe cards from page 79. Or give each student a copy of page 78; then ask her to color and cut apart the booklet pages and staple them in order.

Nancy Karpyk, Weirton Heights School, Weirton, WV

Cherry Delight

Name _____

TEC61214

1

2 — Crush the cracker.

3 — Pour it into the cup.

4 — Measure the pudding. Add it to the cup. (1/3 cup)

5 — Add two spoonfuls pie filling. (Cherry Pie Filling)

6 — Add one spoonful whipped topping. (Whipped Topping)

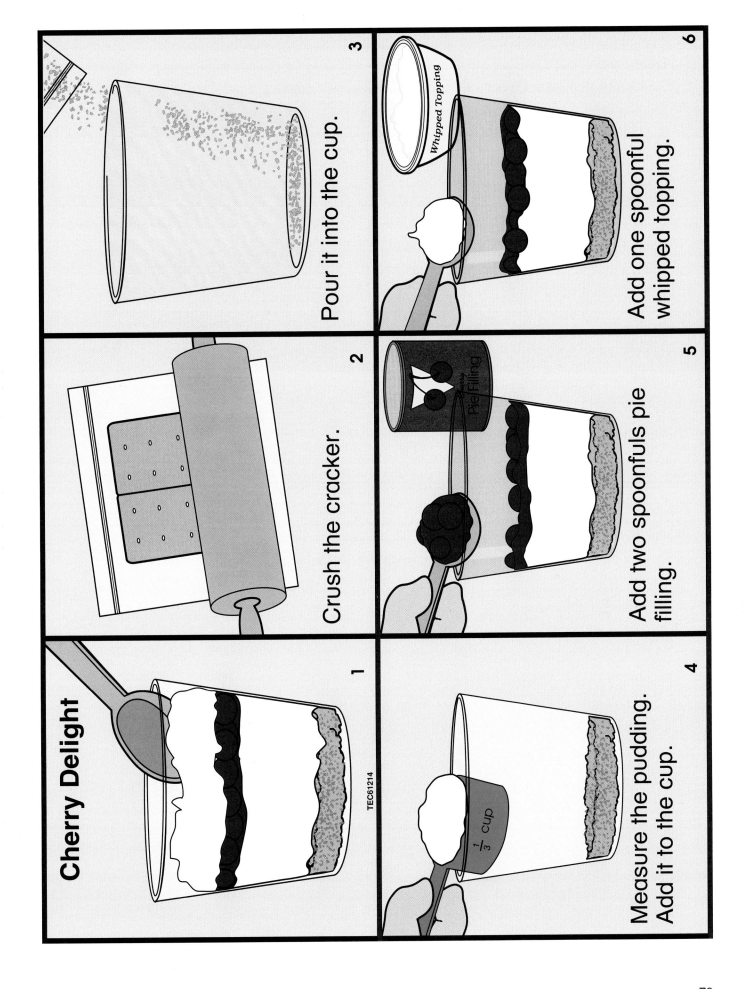

Cherry Delight

TEC61214

1

2

Crush the cracker.

3

Pour it into the cup.

4

Measure the pudding.
Add it to the cup.

$\frac{1}{3}$ cup

5

Add two spoonfuls pie
filling.

Pie Filling

6

Add one spoonful
whipped topping.

Whipped Topping

Dear Parent,

We are making a **Cherry Delight** snack soon. We would be grateful if you could help by providing the following ingredient(s):

_____

_____

_____

We need the ingredient(s) listed above by _____.
                                                                              date

Please let me know if you are able to send the ingredient(s).

Thank you,

_____
                              teacher

- -

Cherry Delight

☐ Yes, I am able to send the ingredient(s).
☐ No, I am unable to send the ingredient(s) this time.

_____
                          parent signature

The Best of The Mailbox® *Kids in the Kitchen* • ©The Mailbox® Books • TEC61214

I Made Cherry Delight in School Today!

My favorite part was _____.

It tasted _____.

This is what it looked like:

Chef's signature: _____

The Best of The Mailbox® *Kids in the Kitchen* • ©The Mailbox® Books • TEC61214

80

Ingredients for one:

mini bagel half (head)
flavored cream cheese
chow mein noodles (mane)
2 M&M's Minis candies (eyes)

Utensils and supplies:

paper plate for each child
plastic knife for each child

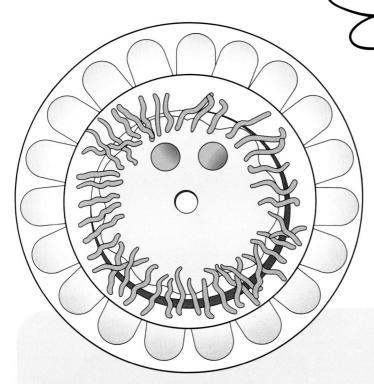

Teacher preparation:

- Arrange the supplies and ingredients for easy student access.
- Display the recipe cards from page 83. Or give each student a copy of page 82; then ask him to color and cut apart the booklet pages and staple them in order.

Amy Rudolph, Lafayette Head Start, Lafayette, IN

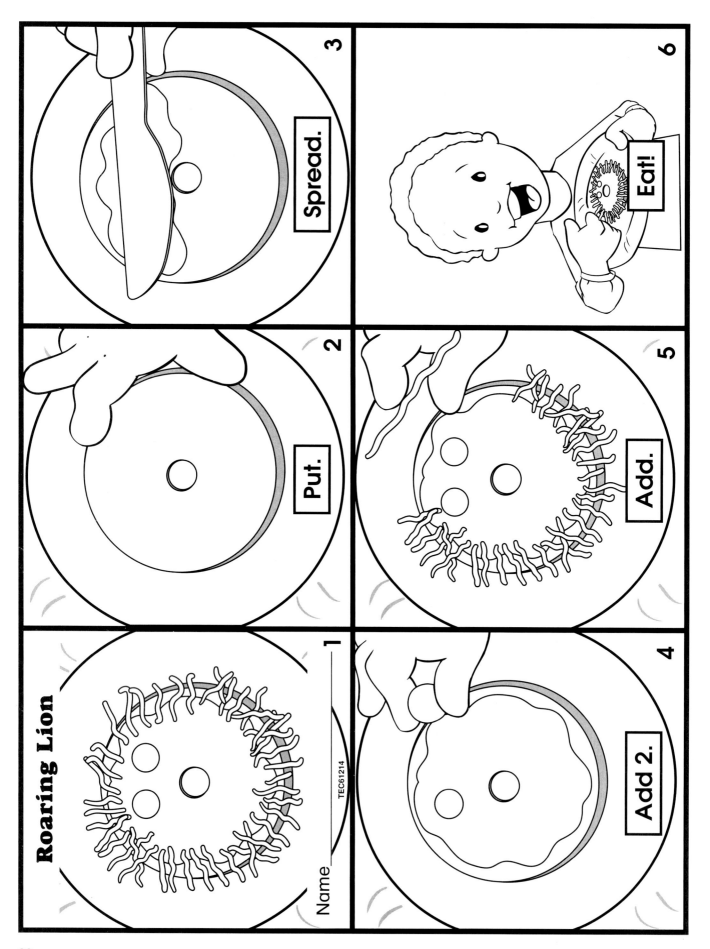

Roaring Lion

Name

Spread.

Put.

Add.

Add 2.

Eat!

1

2

3

4

5

6

TEC61214

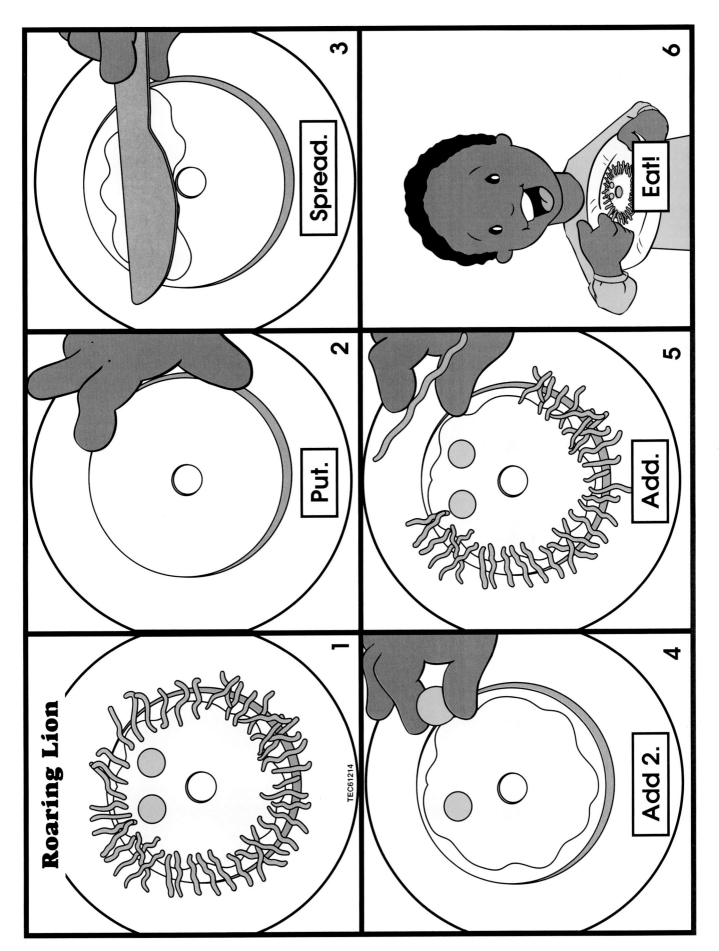

Roaring Lion

TEC61214

1

Put.

2

Spread.

3

Add 2.

4

Add.

5

Eat!

6

Dear Parent,

　　We are making a **Roaring Lion** snack soon. We would be grateful if you could help by providing the following ingredient(s):

_____

_____

_____

We need the ingredient(s) listed above by _____.
　　　　　　　　　　　　　　　　　　　　　　　　　　date

Please let me know if you are able to send the ingredient(s).

　　　　　　　　　Thank you,

　　　　　　_____
　　　　　　　　　　　　　teacher

- -

Roaring Lion

☐ Yes, I am able to send the ingredient(s).

☐ No, I am unable to send the ingredient(s) this time.

　　　　　　　_____
　　　　　　　　　　　　parent signature

I Made a Roaring Lion in School Today!

My favorite part was _____.

It tasted _____.

This is what it looked like:

Chef's signature: _____

Lamb Face

Ingredients for one:

rice cake
soft cream cheese
shredded coconut
3 mini chocolate chips

Utensils and supplies:

napkin for each child
plastic knife for each child
bowl
spoon

Teacher Preparation:

- Arrange the supplies and ingredients for easy student access.
- Display the recipe cards from page 87. Or give each student a copy of page 86; then ask her to color and cut apart the booklet pages and staple them in order.

Brenda Truax

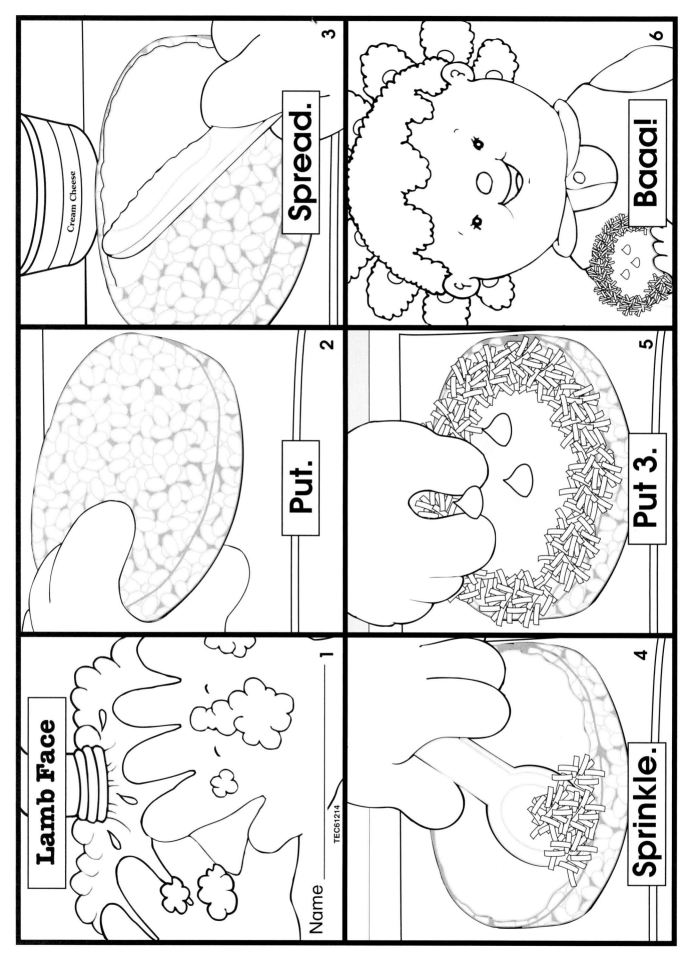

Lamb Face

Name _____

1

Put.

2

Spread.

3

Cream Cheese

Sprinkle.

4

Put 3.

5

Baaa!

6

TEC61214

Dear Parent,

We are making a **Lamb Face** snack soon. We would be grateful if you could help by providing the following ingredient(s):

_____

_____

_____

We need the ingredient(s) listed above by _____.
                                                    date

Please let me know if you are able to send the ingredient(s).

Thank you,

_____
                teacher

- -

Lamb Face

☐ Yes, I am able to send the ingredient(s).

☐ No, I am unable to send the ingredient(s) this time.

_____
            parent signature

I Made a Lamb Face in School Today!

My favorite part was _____.

It tasted _____.

This is what it looked like:

Chef's signature: _____

Cat in the Hat Snack

Ingredients for one:

scoop of vanilla ice cream
mini ice cream cone wrapped with a
   strip of red Fruit by the Foot snack
3 M&M's Minis candies
black decorating gel

Utensils and supplies:

paper plate for each child
plastic spoon for each child

Teacher preparation:

- Use an ice cream scoop to scoop balls of ice cream onto a cookie sheet and then place the sheet in the freezer.
- Cut red Fruit by the Foot snack into four-inch strips. Wrap one strip around each cone.
- Arrange the supplies and ingredients for easy student access.
- Display the recipe cards from page 91. Or give each student a copy of page 90; then ask her to color and cut apart the booklet pages and staple them in order.

Terry Schreiber, Holy Family School, Norwood, NJ

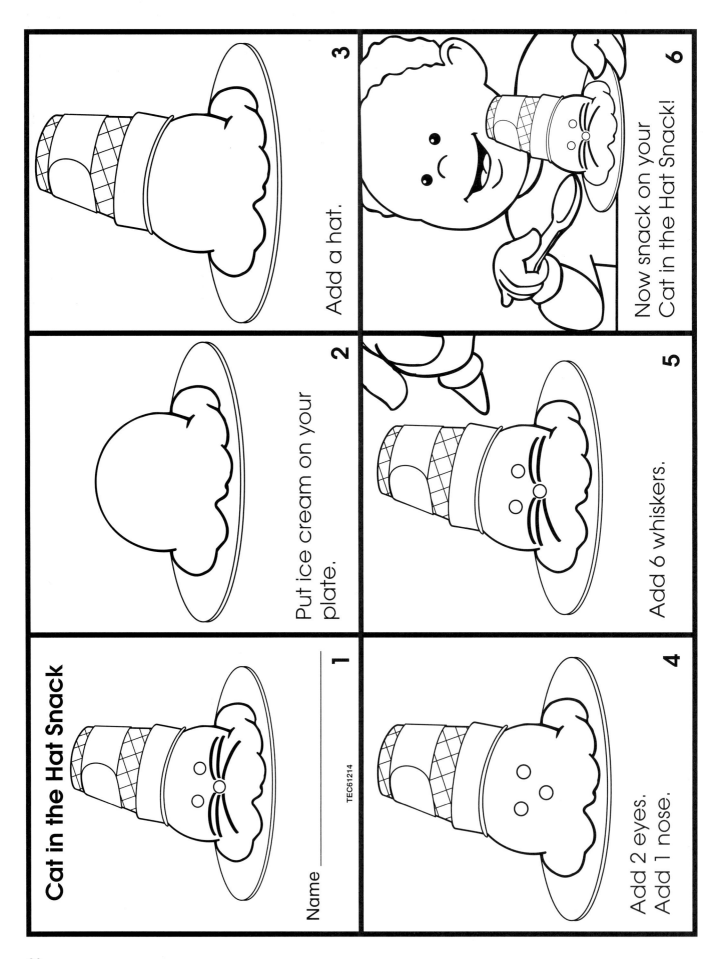

Cat in the Hat Snack

Name _____

TEC61214

1

Put ice cream on your plate.

2

Add a hat.

3

Add 2 eyes.
Add 1 nose.

4

Add 6 whiskers.

5

Now snack on your Cat in the Hat Snack!

6

Cat in the Hat Snack

1

TEC61214

2

Put ice cream on your plate.

3

Add a hat.

4

Add 2 eyes.
Add 1 nose.

5

Add 6 whiskers.

6

Now snack on your Cat in the Hat Snack!

Dear Parent,

   We are making a **Cat in the Hat Snack** soon. We would be grateful if you could help by providing the following ingredient(s):

_____

_____

_____

We need the ingredient(s) listed above by _____.
                                                      date

Please let me know if you are able to send the ingredient(s).

                        Thank you,

                        _____
                                teacher

- -

Cat in the Hat Snack

☐ Yes, I am able to send the ingredient(s).

☐ No, I am unable to send the ingredient(s) this time.

                        _____
                                parent signature

I Made a Cat in the Hat Snack in School Today!

My favorite part was _____.

It tasted _____.

This is what it looked like:

Chef's signature: _____

Ingredients for one:

graham cracker
marshmallow creme
chocolate cookie half
yellow decorating sugar
M&M's Minis candies

Utensils and supplies:

napkin for each child
plastic knife for each child

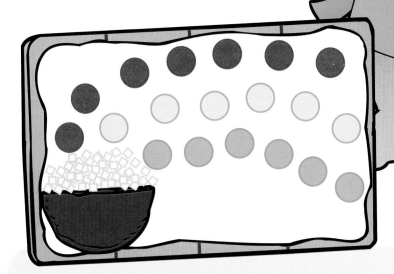

Teacher preparation:

- Break chocolate cookies in half.
- Arrange the supplies and ingredients for easy student access.
- Display the recipe cards from page 95. Or give each student a copy of page 94; then ask her to color and cut apart the booklet pages and staple them in order.

Karen Knipe, Cape Horn Christian Academy, South Williamsport, PA

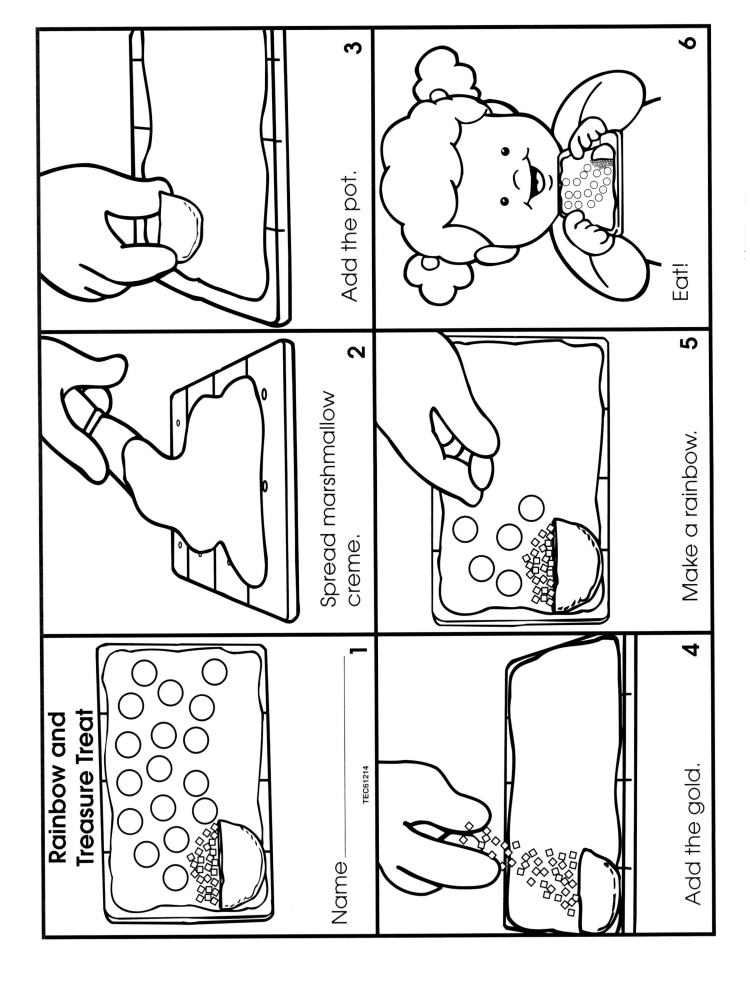

3

Add the pot.

6

Eat!

2

Spread marshmallow creme.

5

Make a rainbow.

Rainbow and Treasure Treat

1

Name _____

TEC61214

4

Add the gold.

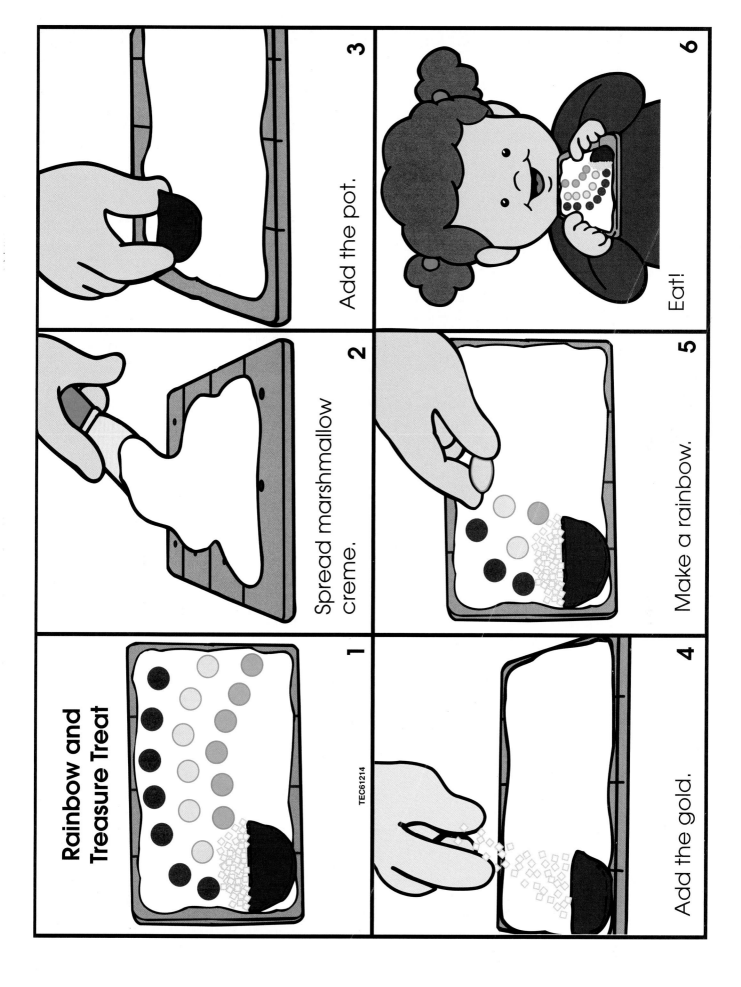

Rainbow and Treasure Treat

1

TEC61214

2

Spread marshmallow creme.

3

Add the pot.

4

Add the gold.

5

Make a rainbow.

6

Eat!

Dear Parent,

    We are making a **Rainbow and Treasure Treat** soon. We would be grateful if you could help by providing the following ingredient(s):

_____

_____

_____

We need the ingredient(s) listed above by _____.
                                                date

Please let me know if you are able to send the ingredient(s).
                   Thank you,

                _____
                           teacher

- -

Rainbow and Treasure Treat

☐ Yes, I am able to send the ingredient(s).
☐ No, I am unable to send the ingredient(s) this time.

                _____
                     parent signature

I Made a Rainbow and Treasure Treat in School Today!

My favorite part was _____.

It tasted _____.

This is what it looked like:

Chef's signature: _____

Gold Coins

Ingredients for one:

3 round crackers
3 thin banana slices
honey
green sugar crystals (lucky dust)

Utensils and supplies:

paper plate for each child

Teacher preparation:

- Arrange the supplies and ingredients for easy student access.
- Display the recipe cards from page 99. Or give each student a copy of page 98; then ask her to color and cut apart the booklet pages and staple them in order.

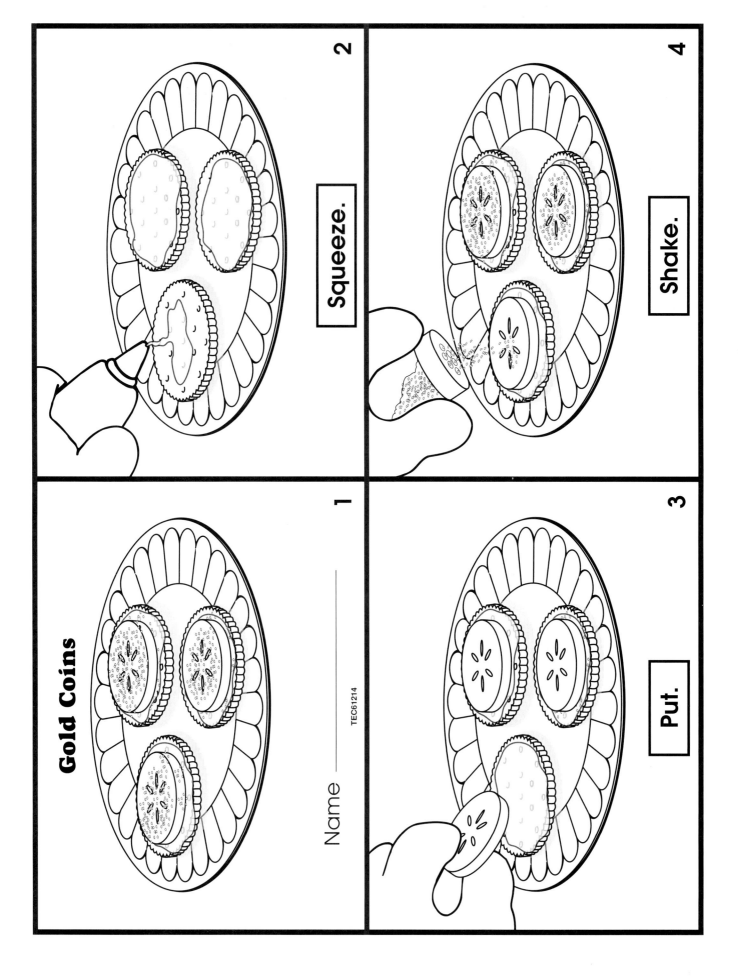

Gold Coins

2 Squeeze.

4 Shake.

1

3 Put.

Name _____

TEC61214

The Best of The Mailbox® *Kids in the Kitchen* • ©The Mailbox® Books • TEC61214

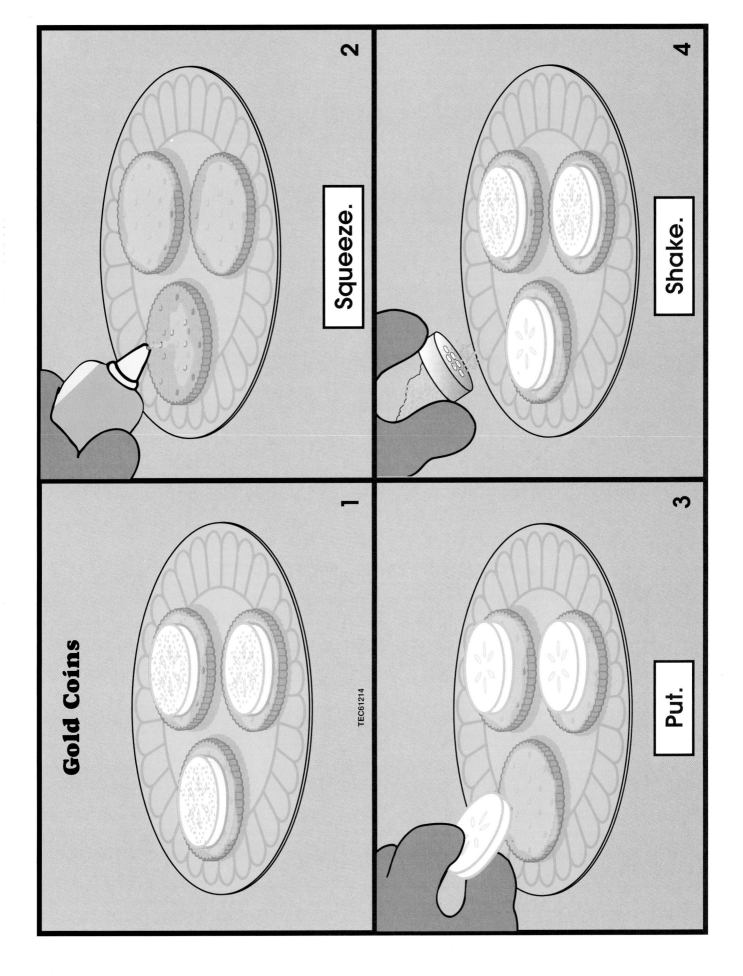

Gold Coins

1

2
Squeeze.

3
Put.

4
Shake.

TEC61214

Dear Parent,

   We are making a **Gold Coin** snack soon. We would be grateful if you could help by providing the following ingredient(s):

_____

_____

_____

We need the ingredient(s) listed above by _____.
                                                          date

Please let me know if you are able to send the ingredient(s).

                    Thank you,

                    _____
                                   teacher

- -

Gold Coin

☐ Yes, I am able to send the ingredient(s).

☐ No, I am unable to send the ingredient(s) this time.

                    _____
                              parent signature

I Made Gold Coins in School Today!

My favorite part was _____.

It tasted _____.

This is what it looked like:

Chef's signature: _____

April Fools' Day Egg

Ingredients for one:

canned-peach half
¼ cup vanilla yogurt

Utensils and supplies:

bowl
spoon
¼ cup measuring cup
small plate for each child
plastic spoon for each child

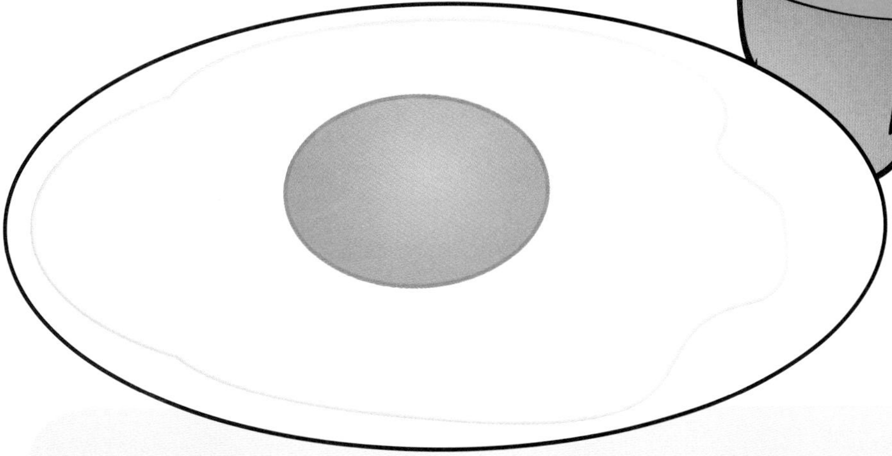

Teacher preparation:

- Arrange the supplies and ingredients for easy student access.
- Display the recipe cards from page 103. Or give each student a copy of page 102; then ask her to color and cut apart the booklet pages and staple them in order.

Charlet Keller • ICC Preschool • Violet Hill, AR

3 Spread.

6 Eat.

2 Scoop.

Vanilla Yogurt

1/4 cup

5 April Fools' Day!

April Fools' Day Egg **1**

Name _____

TEC61214

4 Put.

April Fools' Day Egg

1

2

Vanilla Yogurt

Scoop.

3

Spread.

4

Put.

5

April Fools' Day!

6

Eat.

TEC61214

Dear Parent,

We are making an **April Fools' Day Egg** soon. We would be grateful if you could help by providing the following ingredient(s):

_____

_____

_____

We need the ingredient(s) listed above by _____.

date

Please let me know if you are able to send the ingredient(s).

Thank you,

_____

teacher

April Fools' Day Egg

☐ Yes, I am able to send the ingredient(s).

☐ No, I am unable to send the ingredient(s) this time.

_____

parent signature

I Made an April Fools' Day Egg in School Today!

My favorite part was _____.

It tasted _____.

This is what it looked like:

Chef's signature: _____

Corny Chick

Ingredients for one:

corn muffin
honey butter
2 M&M's Minis candies
cheese triangle

Utensils and supplies:

napkin for each child
plastic knife for each child

Teacher preparation:

- Arrange the supplies and ingredients for easy student access.
- Display the recipe cards from page 107. Or give each student a copy of page 106; then ask her to color and cut apart the booklet pages and staple them in order.

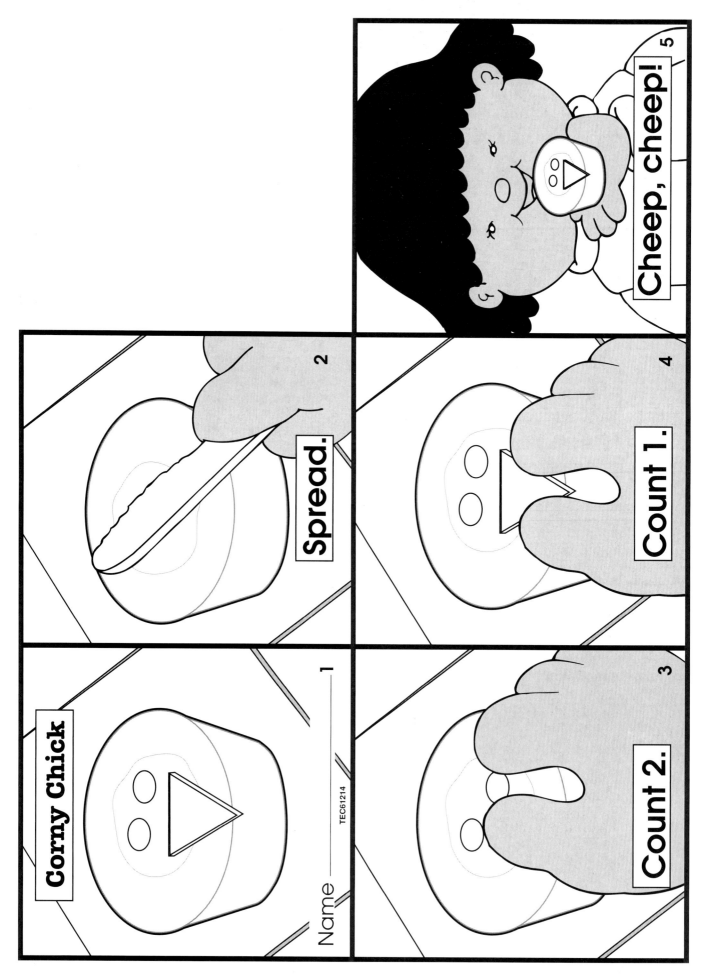

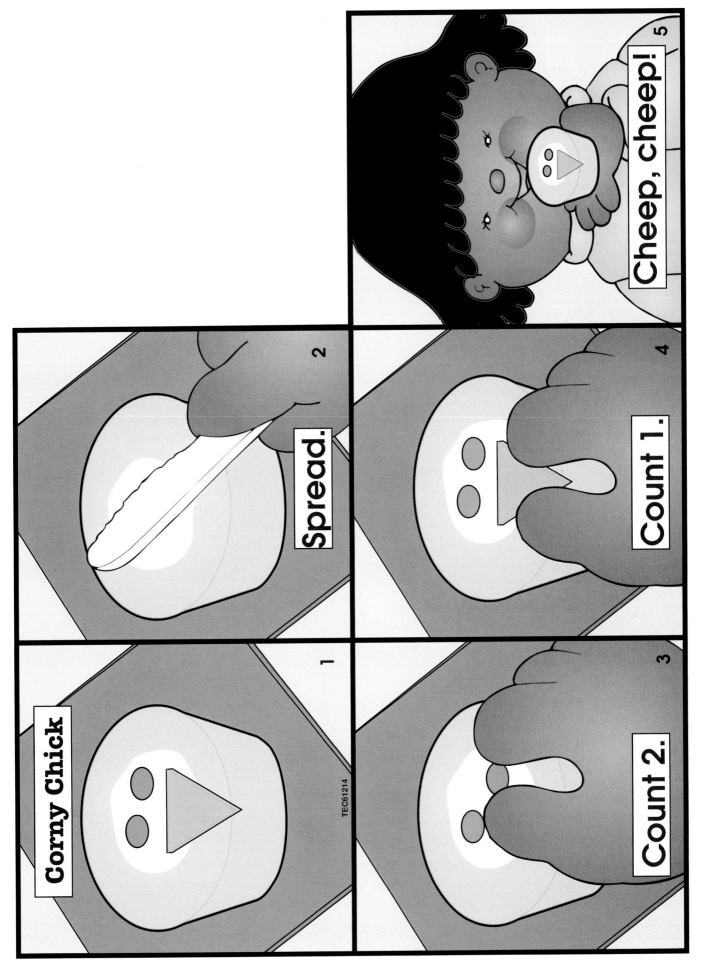

Dear Parent,
   We are making a **Corny Chick** snack soon. We would be grateful if you could help by providing the following ingredient(s):

_____

_____

_____
We need the ingredient(s) listed above by _____.
                                                    date

Please let me know if you are able to send the ingredient(s).
                    Thank you,

                    _____
                                    teacher

- -

Corny Chick

☐ Yes, I am able to send the ingredient(s).
☐ No, I am unable to send the ingredient(s) this time.

                    _____
                                parent signature

I Made a Corny Chick Snack in School Today!

My favorite part was _____.

It tasted _____.

This is what it looked like:

Chef's signature: _____

Ingredients for one:

½ c. chocolate pudding (mud)
2 graham cracker sections (boot tops)
2 Vienna Fingers creme-filled
  sandwich cookie halves
  (boot bottoms)

Utensils and supplies:

disposable bowl for each child
plastic spoon for each child
½ c. measuring cup

Teacher preparation:

- Arrange the supplies and ingredients for easy student access.
- Display the recipe cards from page 111. Or give each student a copy of page 110; then ask him to color and cut apart the booklet pages and staple them in order.

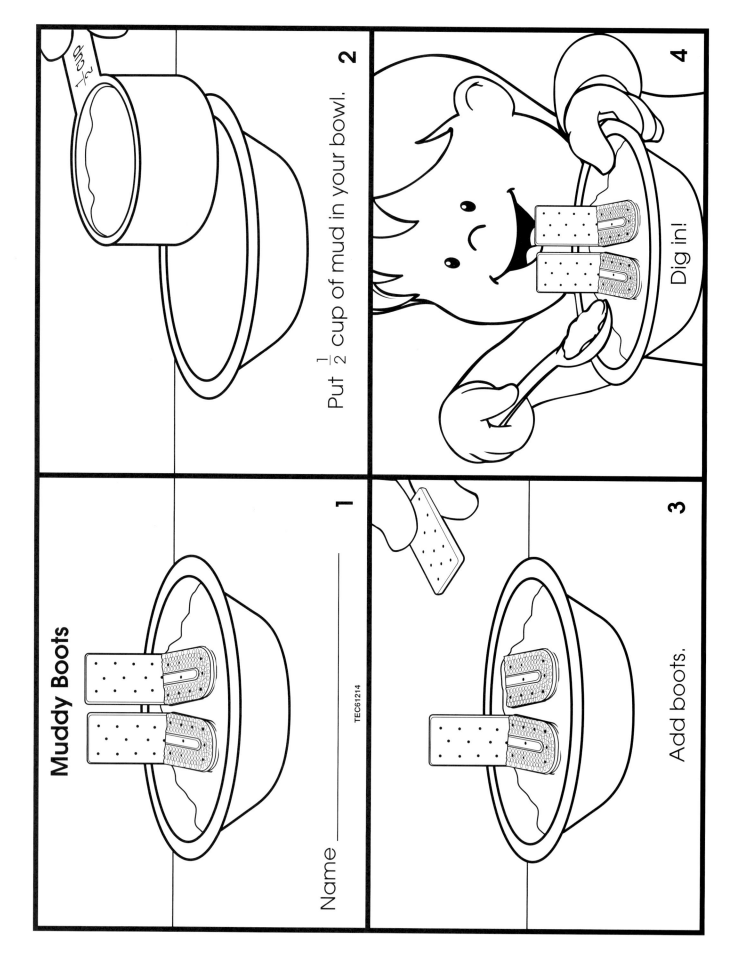

Muddy Boots

1

Name _____

TEC61214

2

Put $\frac{1}{2}$ cup of mud in your bowl.

3

Add boots.

4

Dig in!

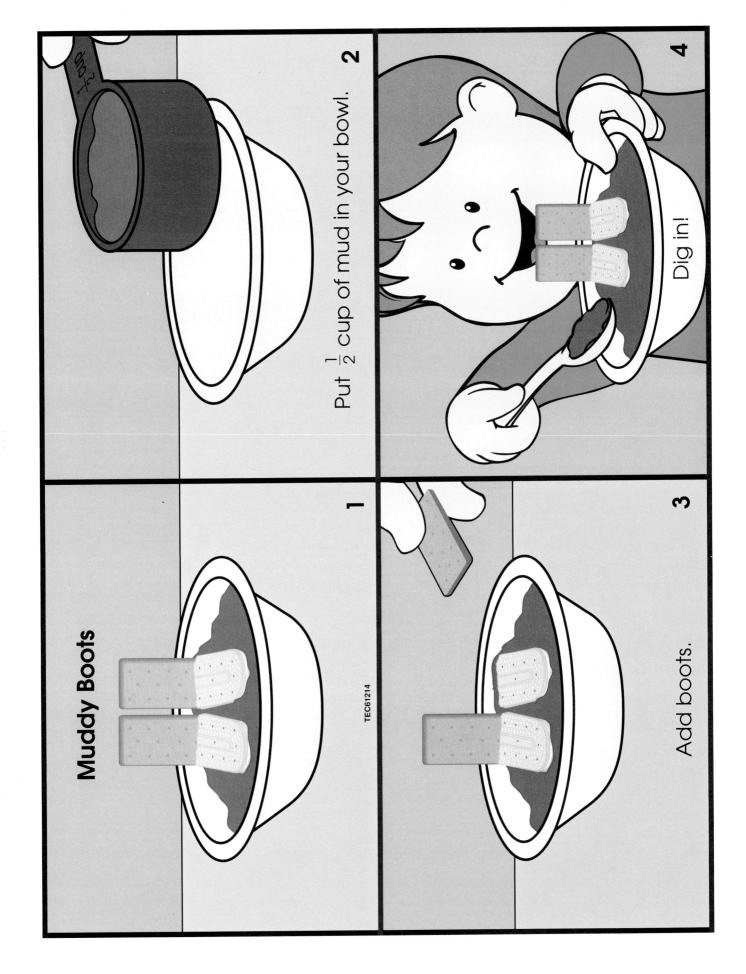

Muddy Boots

TEC61214

2

Put $\frac{1}{2}$ cup of mud in your bowl.

1

3

Add boots.

4

Dig in!

Dear Parent,

We are making a **Muddy Boots** snack soon. We would be grateful if you could help by providing the following ingredient(s):

_____

_____

_____

We need the ingredient(s) listed above by _____.

                                                                                    date

Please let me know if you are able to send the ingredient(s).

Thank you,

_____

                                                                          teacher

- -

Muddy Boots

☐ Yes, I am able to send the ingredient(s).

☐ No, I am unable to send the ingredient(s) this time.

_____

                                                                     parent signature

---

I Made Muddy Boots in School Today!

My favorite part was _____.

It tasted _____.

This is what it looked like:

Chef's signature: _____

Caterpillar Roll-Up

Ingredients for one:

slice of bread, crust removed
whipped cream cheese, tinted green
decorating gel

Utensils and supplies:

piece of waxed paper for each child
rolling pin
plastic knife for each child
small disposable plate for each child

Teacher preparation:

- Arrange the supplies and ingredients for easy student access.
- Display the recipe cards from page 115. Or give each student a copy of page 114; then ask her to color and cut apart the booklet pages and staple them in order.

adapted from an idea by Virginia Zeletzki, Banyan Creek Elementary, Delray Beach, FL

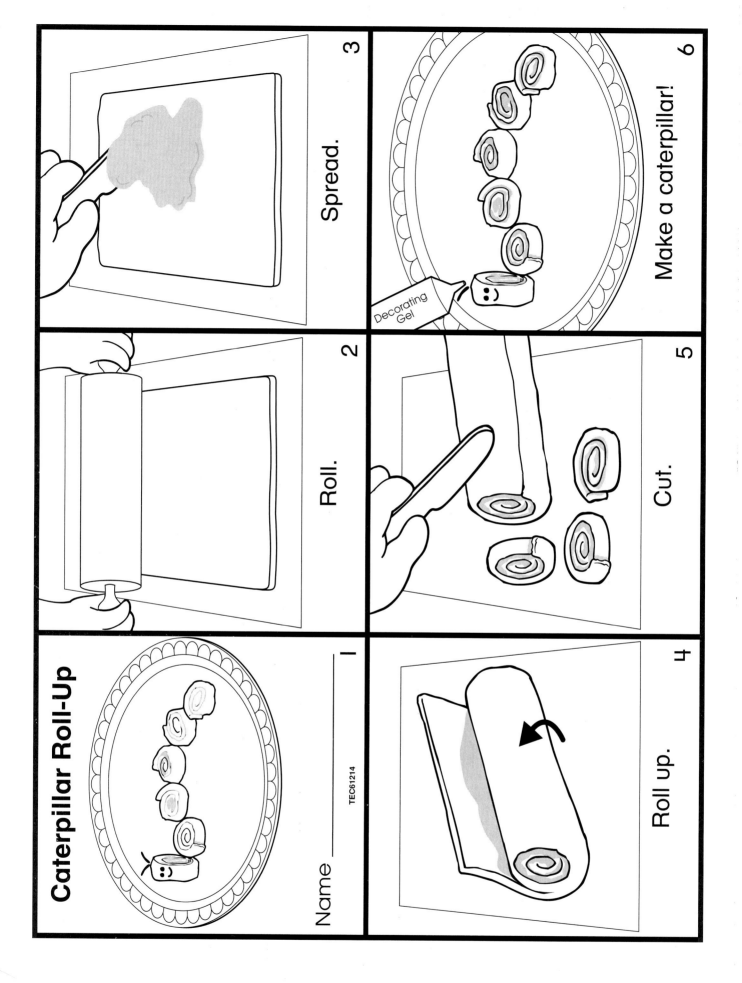

Caterpillar Roll-Up

Name _____

TEC61214

1

2

Roll.

3

Spread.

4

Roll up.

5

Cut.

6

Make a caterpillar!

Decorating Gel

Caterpillar Roll-Up

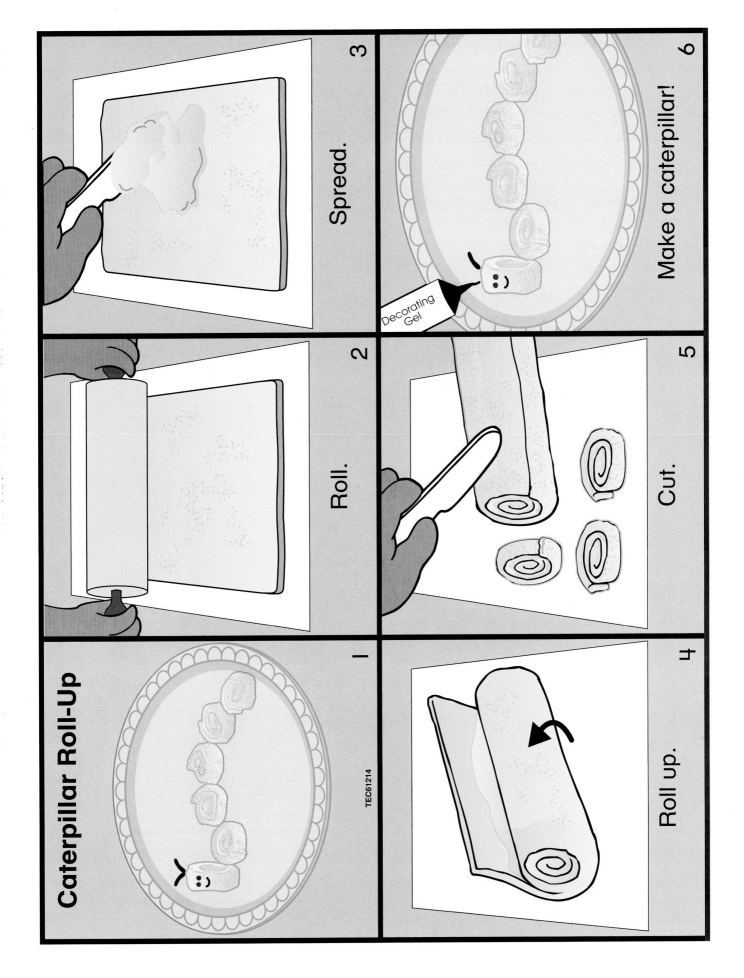

1

TEC61214

2

Roll.

3

Spread.

4

Roll up.

5

Cut.

6

Make a caterpillar!

Decorating Gel

Dear Parent,

   We are making a **Caterpillar Roll-up** snack soon. We would be grateful if you could help by providing the following ingredient(s):

_____

_____

_____

We need the ingredient(s) listed above by _____.
                                              date

Please let me know if you are able to send the ingredient(s).
                              Thank you,

                    _____
                                teacher

- -

Caterpillar Roll-up

☐ Yes, I am able to send the ingredient(s).

☐ No, I am unable to send the ingredient(s) this time.

                    _____
                              parent signature

I Made a Caterpillar Roll-up in School Today!

My favorite part was _____.

It tasted _____.

This is what it looked like:

Chef's signature: _____

Delicious Lily Pad

Ingredients for one:

slice-and-bake sugar cookie dough
green-tinted icing
flower-shaped cake decoration

Utensils and supplies:

paper plate for each child
jumbo craft stick for each child
knife *(for teacher use only)*
oven *(for teacher use only)*

Teacher preparation:

- Slice sugar cookie dough; then cut out a small triangle shape from each slice to create a lily pad. Bake the cookies as directed on the package.
- Arrange the supplies and ingredients for easy student access.
- Display the recipe cards from page 119. Or give each student a copy of page 118; then ask her to color and cut apart the booklet pages and staple them in order.

Lari Junkin, Cathedral School, Natchez, MS

2

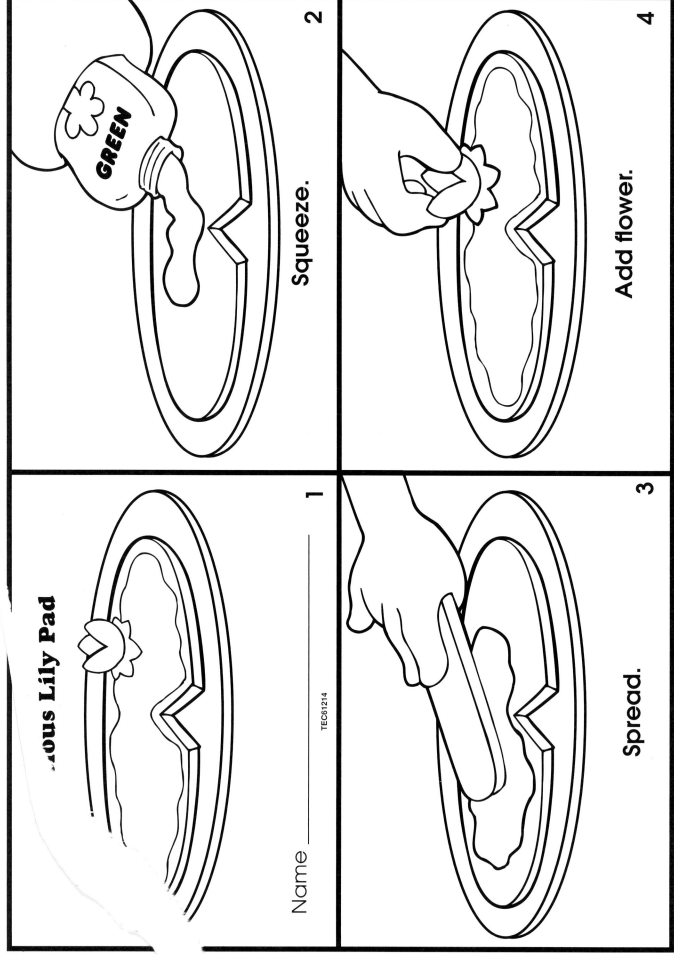

Squeeze.

4

Add flower.

...ous Lily Pad

1

Name _____

3

Spread.

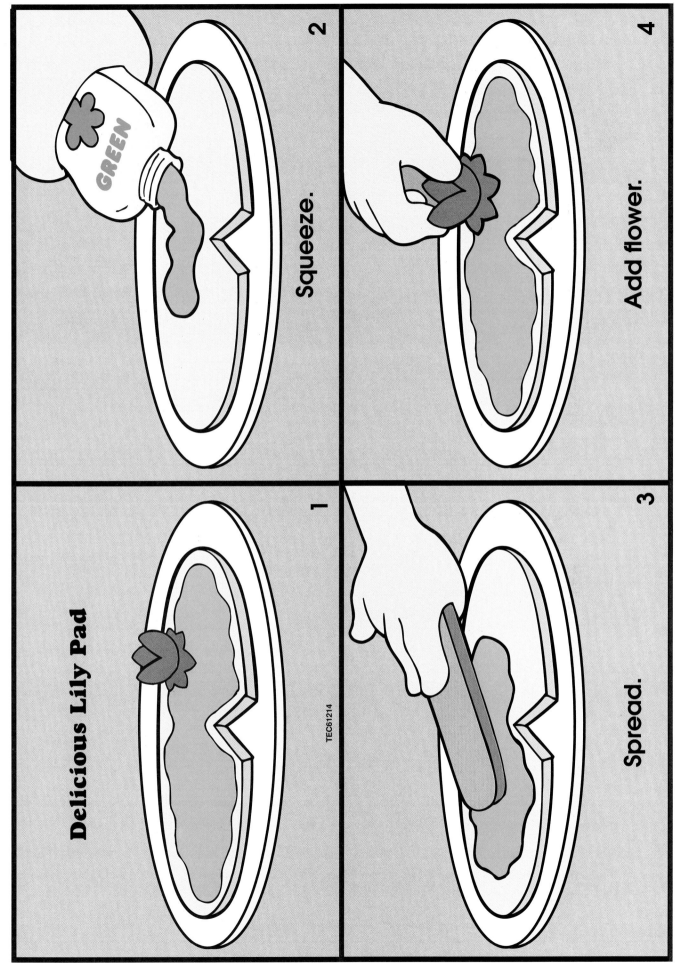

Delicious Lily Pad

1

2

Squeeze.

3

Spread.

4

Add flower.

TEC61214

Dear Parent,

We are making a **Delicious Lily Pad** snack soon. We would be grateful if you could help by providing the following ingredient(s):

_____

_____

_____

We need the ingredient(s) listed above by _____.
　　　　　　　　　　　　　　　　　　　　　　　　　　　　　　date

Please let me know if you are able to send the ingredient(s).
　　　　　　　　　　　　　Thank you,

_____
　　　　　　　　　　　　　　　　teacher

- -

Delicious Lily Pad

☐ Yes, I am able to send the ingredient(s).
☐ No, I am unable to send the ingredient(s) this time.

_____
　　　　　　　　　　　　　　　parent signature

I Made a Delicious Lily Pad in School Today!

My favorite part was _____.

It tasted _____.

This is what it looked like:

Chef's signature: _____

Cinco de Mayo Snack

Ingredients for one:

flour tortilla
shredded cheese
mild salsa

Utensils and supplies:

star-shaped cookie cutter (a
  metal one works best)
toaster oven
spoon
paper plate for each child
napkins

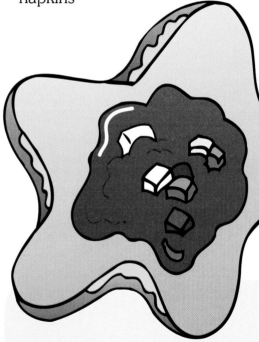

Teacher preparation:

- Arrange the supplies and ingredients for easy student access.
- Display the recipe cards from page 123. Or give each student a
  copy of page 122; then ask him to color and cut apart the booklet
  pages and staple them in order.

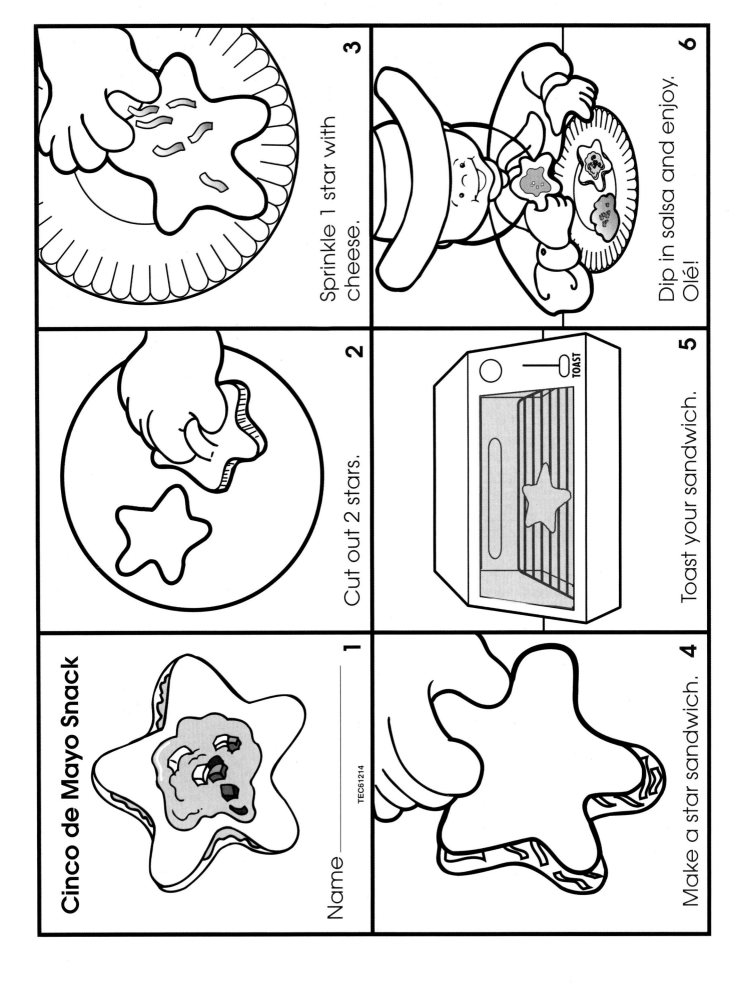

Cinco de Mayo Snack

3 Sprinkle 1 star with cheese.

6 Dip in salsa and enjoy. Olé!

2 Cut out 2 stars.

5 Toast your sandwich.

Name _____

TEC61214

1

4 Make a star sandwich.

Cinco de Mayo Snack

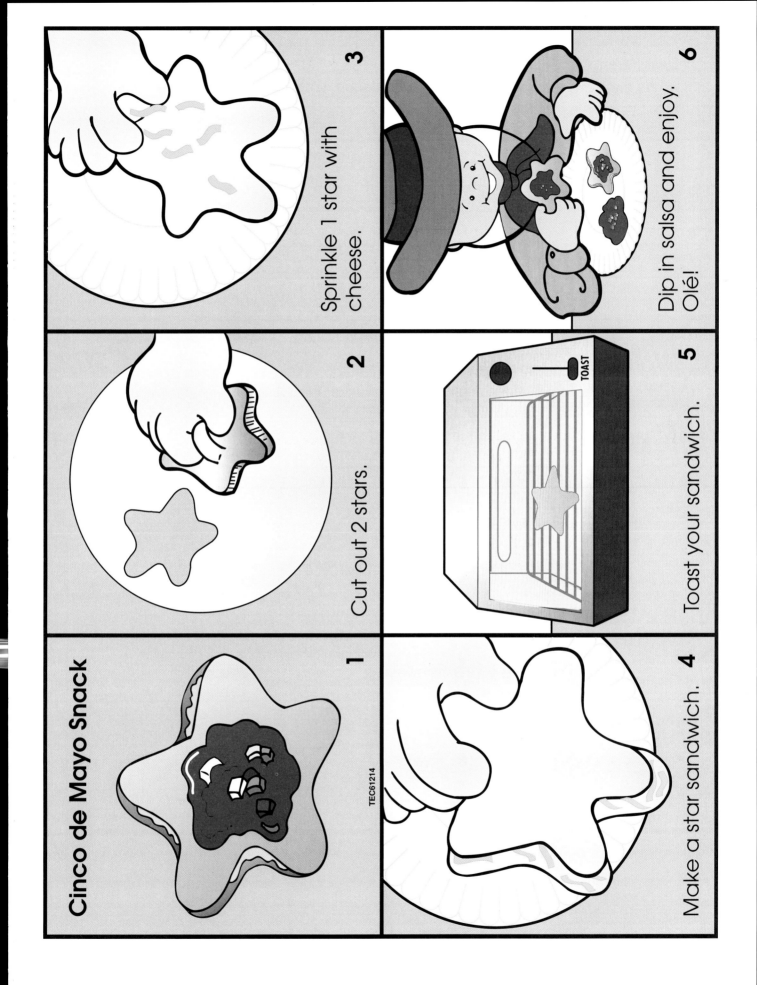

1

2 Cut out 2 stars.

3 Sprinkle 1 star with cheese.

4 Make a star sandwich.

5 Toast your sandwich.

6 Dip in salsa and enjoy. Olé!

TEC61214

Dear Parent,

We are making a **Cinco de Mayo Snack** soon. We would be grateful if you could help by providing the following ingredient(s):

_____

_____

_____

We need the ingredient(s) listed above by _____.

date

Please let me know if you are able to send the ingredient(s).

Thank you,

_____

teacher

Cinco de Mayo Snack

☐ Yes, I am able to send the ingredient(s).

☐ No, I am unable to send the ingredient(s).

_____

parent signature

I Made a Cinco de Mayo Snack in School Today!

My favorite part was _____.

It tasted _____.

This is what it looked like:

Chef's signature: _____

"Berry" Good Pizza

Ingredients for one:

English muffin half
strawberry cream cheese
2 thin strawberry slices
2 thin banana slices
2 blueberries
diluted lemon juice (optional)

Utensils and supplies:

3 bowls
3 spoons
paper plate for each child
plastic knife

Teacher preparation:

- Arrange the supplies and ingredients for easy student access.
- Display the recipe cards from page 127. Or give each student a copy of page 126; then ask her to color and cut apart the booklet pages and staple them in order.

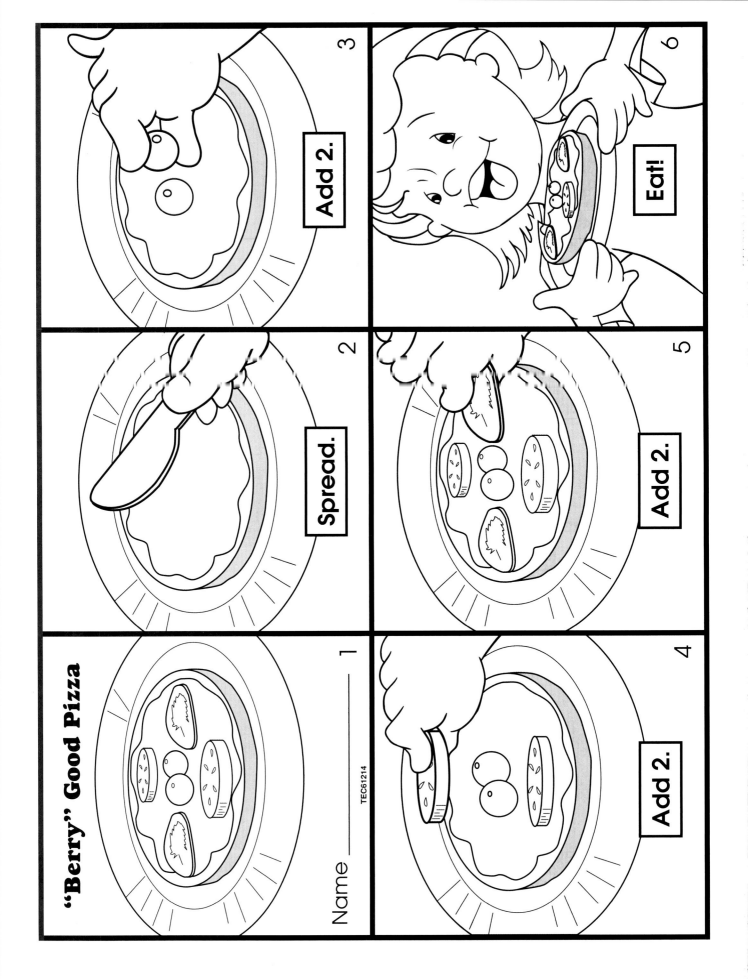

3

Add 2.

6

Eat!

2

Spread.

5

Add 2.

"Berry" Good Pizza

1

Name _____

TEC61214

4

Add 2.

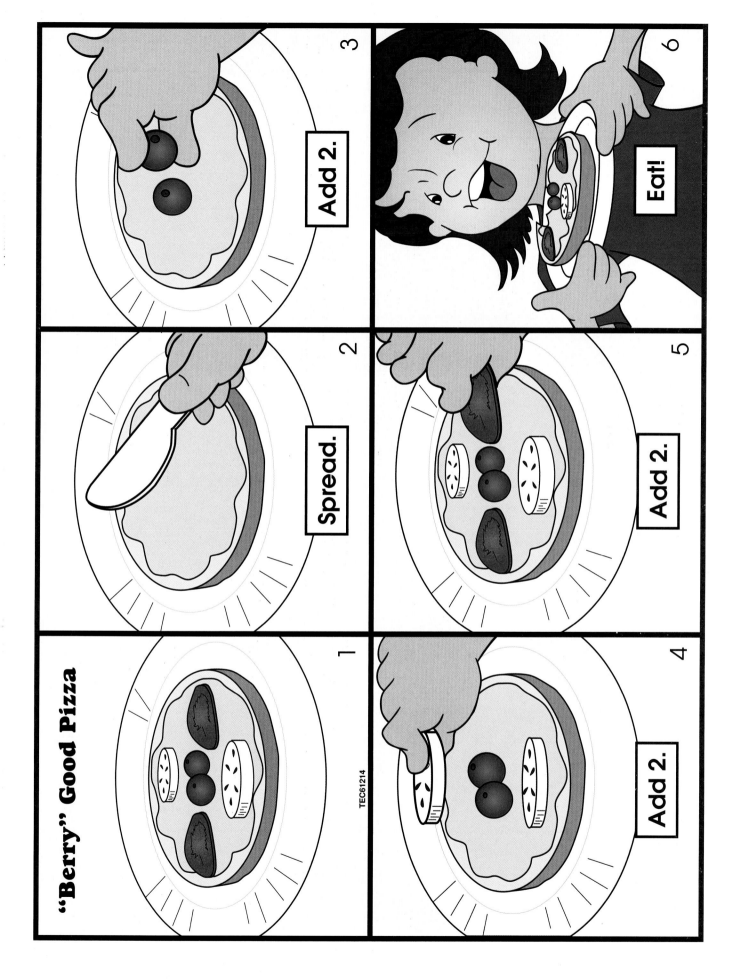

Dear Parent,
    We are making a **"Berry" Good Pizza** snack soon. We would be grateful if you could help by providing the following ingredient(s):

_____

_____

_____

We need the ingredient(s) listed above by _____.
                                                            date

Please let me know if you are able to send the ingredient(s).
                    Thank you,

                    _____
                                    teacher

- -

"Berry" Good Pizza

☐ Yes, I am able to send the ingredient(s).
☐ No, I am unable to send the ingredient(s) this time.

                    _____
                                    parent signature

I Made "Berry" Good Pizza in School Today!

My favorite part was _____.

It tasted _____.

This is what it looked like:

Chef's signature: _____

Strawberry Double-Dip

Ingredients for one:

2 strawberries
whipped topping
graham cracker crumbs

Utensils and supplies:

2 serving bowls
2 spoons
two 3-oz. paper cups for each
child

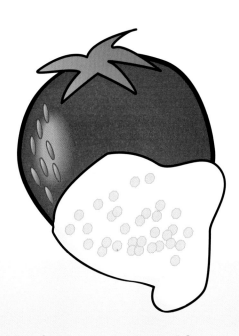

Teacher preparation:

- Arrange the supplies and ingredients for easy student access.
- Display the recipe cards from page 131. Or give each student a
  copy of page 130; then ask her to color and cut apart the booklet
  pages and staple them in order.

Dear Parent,
    We are making a **Strawberry Double-Dip** snack soon. We would be grateful if you could help by providing the following ingredient(s):

_____

_____

_____
We need the ingredient(s) listed above by _____.
                                                          date

Please let me know if you are able to send the ingredient(s).
                        Thank you,

                        _____
                                          teacher

- -

Strawberry Double-Dip

☐ Yes, I am able to send the ingredient(s).
☐ No, I am unable to send the ingredient(s) this time.

                        _____
                                    parent signature

I Made a Strawberry Double-Dip in School Today!

My favorite part was _____.

It tasted _____.

This is what it looked like:

Chef's signature: _____

Sunshine Salad

Ingredients for one:

spoonful of lemon yogurt
8 pineapple tidbits

Utensils and supplies:

paper plate for each child
plastic spoon for each child

Teacher preparation:

- Arrange the supplies and ingredients for easy student access.
- Display the recipe cards from page 135. Or give each student a copy of page 134; then ask her to color and cut apart the booklet pages and staple them in order.

adapted from an idea by Samantha Towne, Cordova, TN

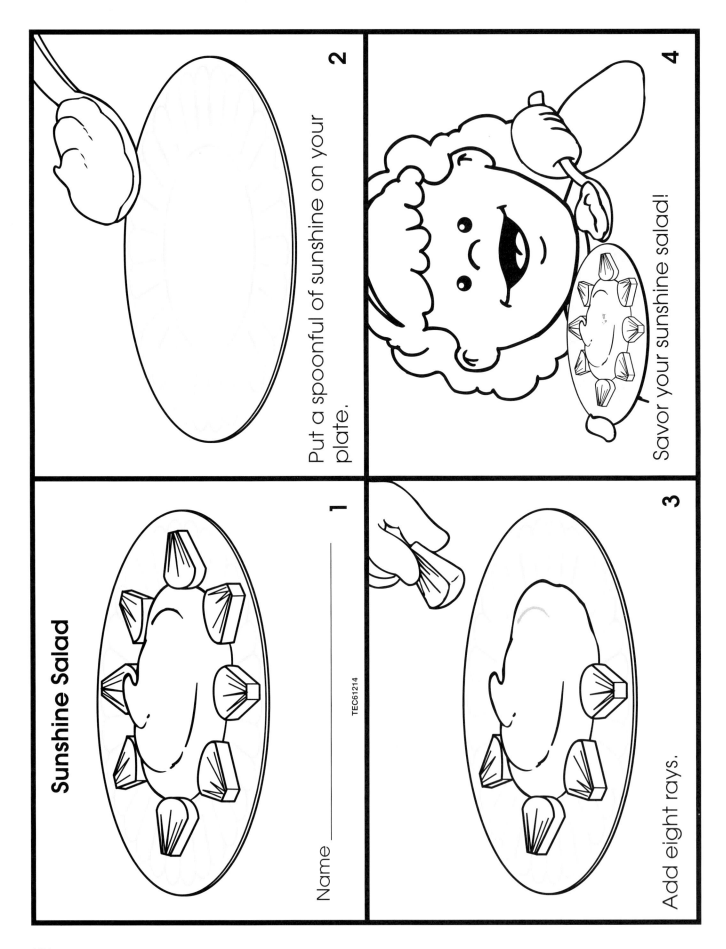

Sunshine Salad

1

Name _____

TEC61214

2

Put a spoonful of sunshine on your plate.

3

Add eight rays.

4

Savor your sunshine salad!

Sunshine Salad

1

2

Put a spoonful of sunshine on your plate.

TEC61214

3

Add eight rays.

4

Savor your sunshine salad!

Dear Parent,

We are making a **Sunshine Salad** snack soon. We would be grateful if you could help by providing the following ingredient(s):

_____

_____

_____

We need the ingredient(s) listed above by _____.

date

Please let me know if you are able to send the ingredient(s).

Thank you,

_____

teacher

- -

Sunshine Salad

☐ Yes, I am able to send the ingredient(s).

☐ No, I am unable to send the ingredient(s) this time.

_____

parent signature

I Made Sunshine Salad in School Today!

My favorite part was _____.

It tasted _____.

This is what it looked like:

Chef's signature: _____

Ingredients for one:

slice of bread
softened butter
cinnamon sugar

Utensils and supplies:

napkin per child
star-shaped cookie cutter
plastic knife per child
shaker
toaster oven

Teacher preparation:

- Arrange the supplies and ingredients for easy student access.
- Display the recipe cards from page 139. Or give each student a copy of page 138; then ask him to color and cut apart the booklet pages and staple them in order.

Karen Smith, Pace, FL

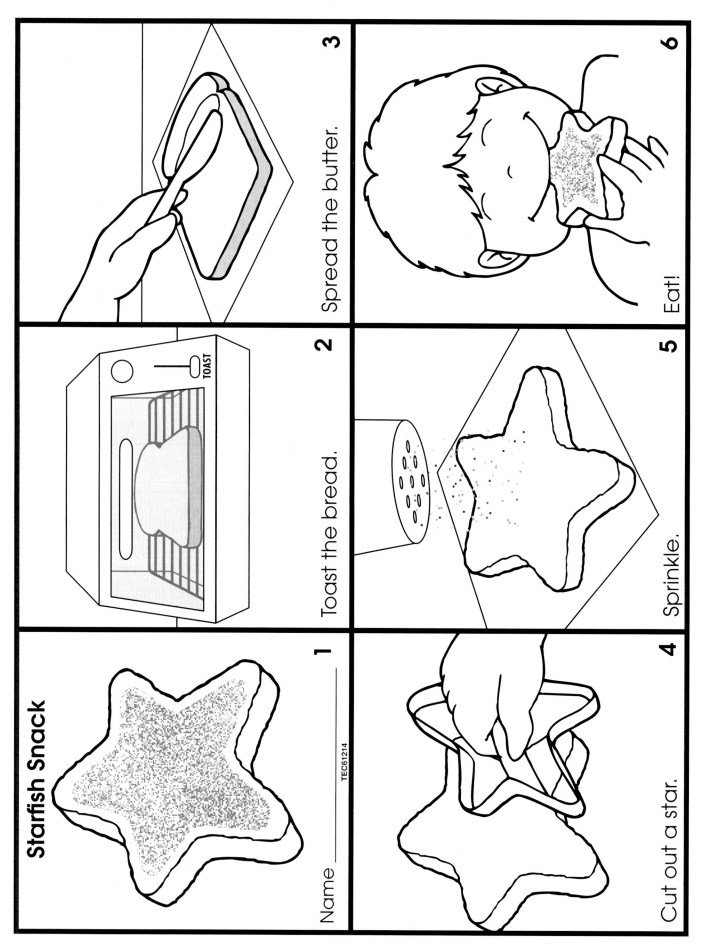

3

Spread the butter.

6

Eat!

2

Toast the bread.

5

Sprinkle.

Starfish Snack

1

Name _____

TEC61214

4

Cut out a star.

The Best of The Mailbox® *Kids in the Kitchen* • ©The Mailbox® Books • TEC61214

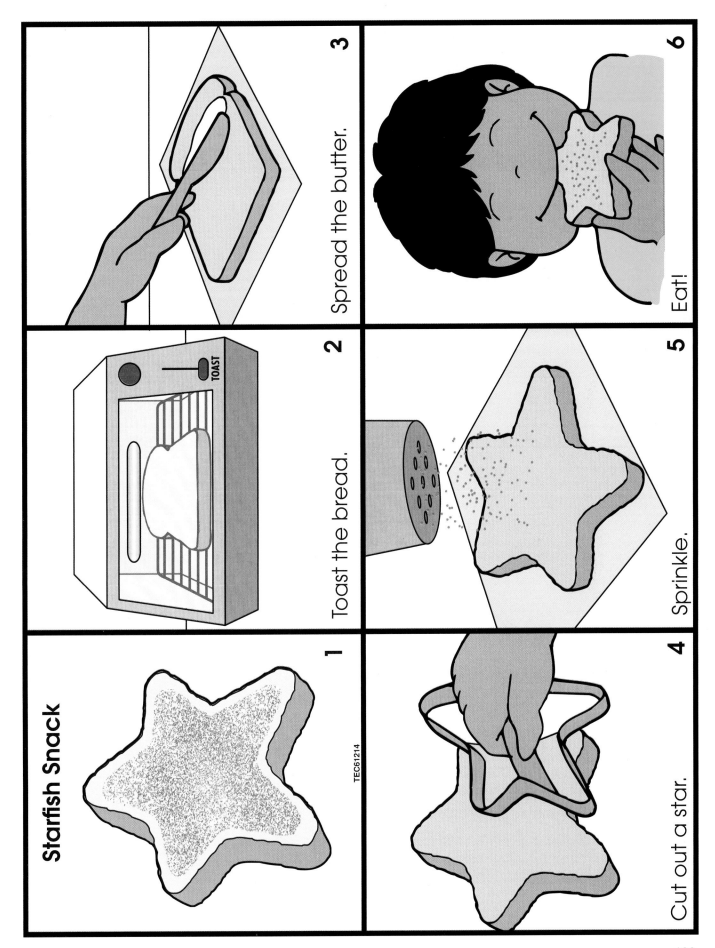

Starfish Snack 1

2 Toast the bread.

3 Spread the butter.

4 Cut out a star.

5 Sprinkle.

6 Eat!

TOAST

TEC61214

Dear Parent,
   We are making a **Starfish Snack** soon. We would be grateful if you could help by providing the following ingredient(s):

_____

_____

_____

We need the ingredient(s) listed above by _____.
                                                                    date

Please let me know if you are able to send the ingredient(s).
                    Thank you,

                    _____
                                    teacher

- -

Starfish Snack

☐ Yes, I am able to send the ingredient(s).
☐ No, I am unable to send the ingredient(s) this time.

                    _____
                              parent signature

I Made a Starfish Snack in School Today!

My favorite part was _____.

It tasted _____.

This is what it looked like:

Chef's signature: _____

Seashells and Seaweed

Ingredients for one:

cooked shell pasta, served warm (seashells)
shredded mozzarella cheese, tinted green (seaweed)
butter
salt

Utensils and supplies:

small ladle
spoon
plastic butter knife
disposable bowl for each child
plastic spoon for each child
napkin for each child

Teacher preparation:

- Arrange the supplies and ingredients for easy student access.
- Display the recipe cards from page 143. Or give each student a copy of page 142; then ask her to color and cut apart the booklet pages and staple them in order.

Mary D. Bond, Airline Baptist Church Child Development Center, Bossier City, LA

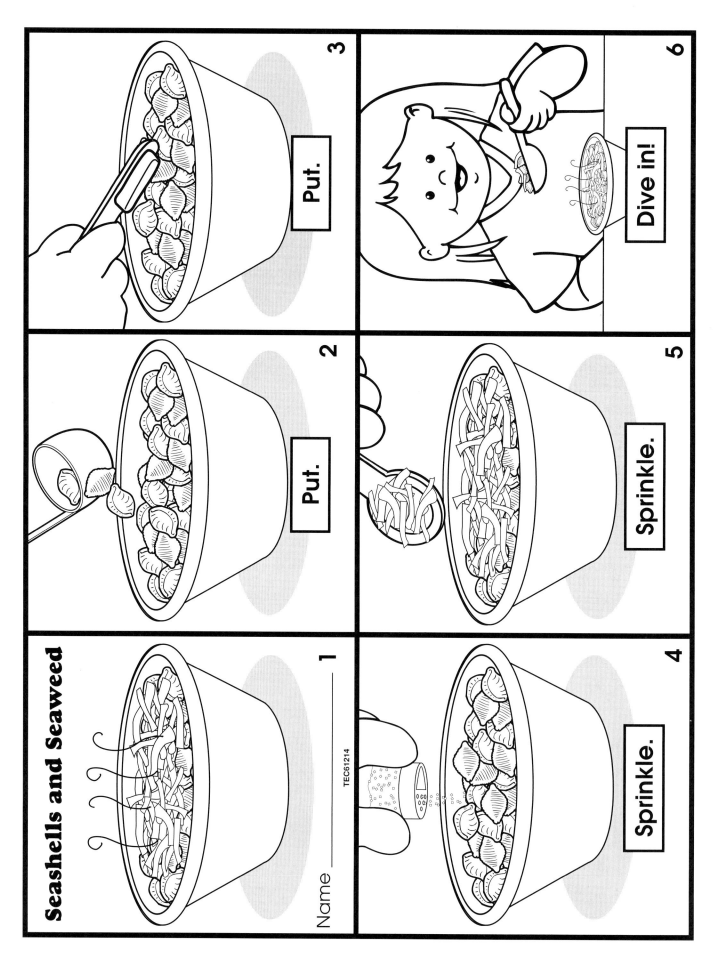

Seashells and Seaweed

Name _____

1

2

Put.

3

Put.

4

Sprinkle.

5

Sprinkle.

6

Dive in!

TEC61214

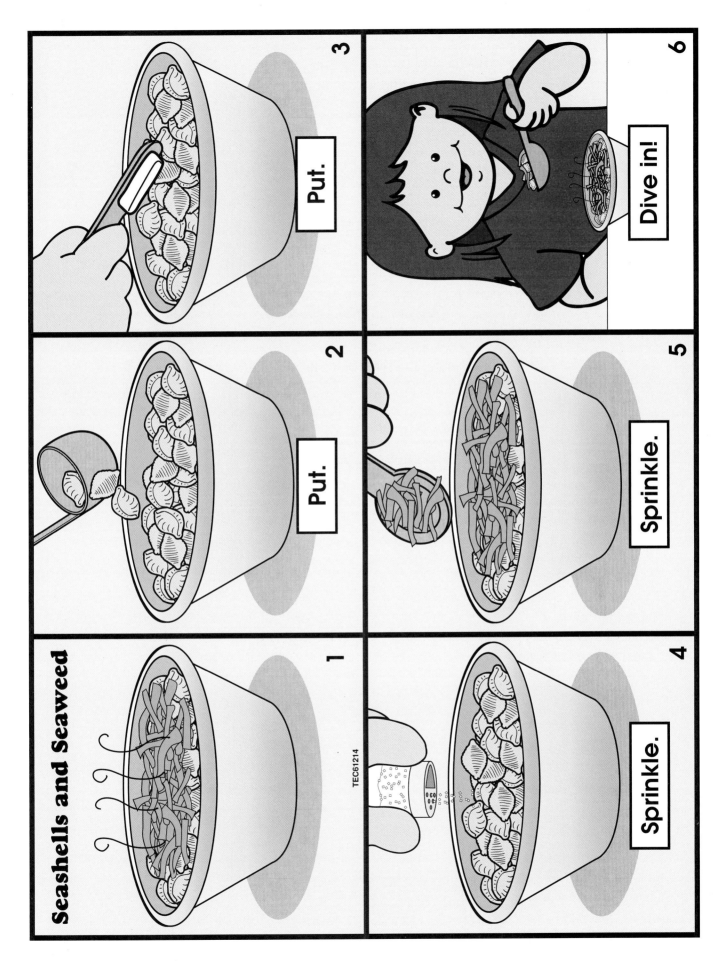

Seashells and Seaweed

1

2 Put.

3 Put.

4 Sprinkle.

5 Sprinkle.

6 Dive in!

TEC61214

Dear Parent,

We are making a **Seashells and Seaweed** snack soon. We would be grateful if you could help by providing the following ingredient(s):

_____

_____

_____

We need the ingredient(s) listed above by _____.
                                                                    date

Please let me know if you are able to send the ingredient(s).

Thank you,

_____
                        teacher

- -

Seashells and Seaweed

☐ Yes, I am able to send the ingredient(s).
☐ No, I am unable to send the ingredient(s) this time.

_____
                        parent signature

I Made Seashells and Seaweed in School Today!

My favorite part was _____.

It tasted _____.

This is what it looked like:

Chef's signature: _____

Independence Day Tart

Ingredients for one:

single-serving sponge cake
whipped topping
sliced strawberries
blueberries

Utensils and supplies:

paper plate for each child
spoon for each child
serving spoons for topping and berries

Teacher preparation:

- Arrange the supplies and ingredients for easy student access.
- Display the recipe cards from page 147. Or give each student a copy of page 146; then ask her to color and cut apart the booklet pages and staple them in order.

Independence Day Tart

1

Name _____

TEC61214

2

Spread whipped topping on cake.

3

Arrange strawberries.

4

Arrange blueberries.

5

Add more topping.

6

Enjoy!

The Best of The Mailbox® *Kids in the Kitchen* • ©The Mailbox® Books • TEC61214

Independence Day Tart

1

TEC61214

2 Spread whipped topping on cake.

3 Arrange strawberries.

4 Arrange blueberries.

5 Add more topping.

6 Enjoy!

Dear Parent,

We are making an **Independence Day Tart** snack soon. We would be grateful if you could help by providing the following ingredient(s):

_____

_____

_____

We need the ingredient(s) listed above by _____.
                                                            date

Please let me know if you are able to send the ingredient(s).

Thank you,

_____
                              teacher

- -

Independence Day Tart

☐ Yes, I am able to send the ingredient(s).
☐ No, I am unable to send the ingredient(s) this time.

_____
                          parent signature

I Made an Independence Day Tart in School Today!

My favorite part was _____.

It tasted _____.

This is what it looked like:

Chef's signature: _____

Ingredients for one:

scoop rainbow sherbet
raspberry-lime seltzer
rainbow sprinkles

Utensils and supplies:

plastic cup for each child
spoon for each child
ice cream scoop

Teacher preparation:

- Arrange the supplies and ingredients for easy student access.
- Display the recipe cards from page 151. Or give each student a copy of page 150; then ask her to color and cut apart the booklet pages and staple them in order.

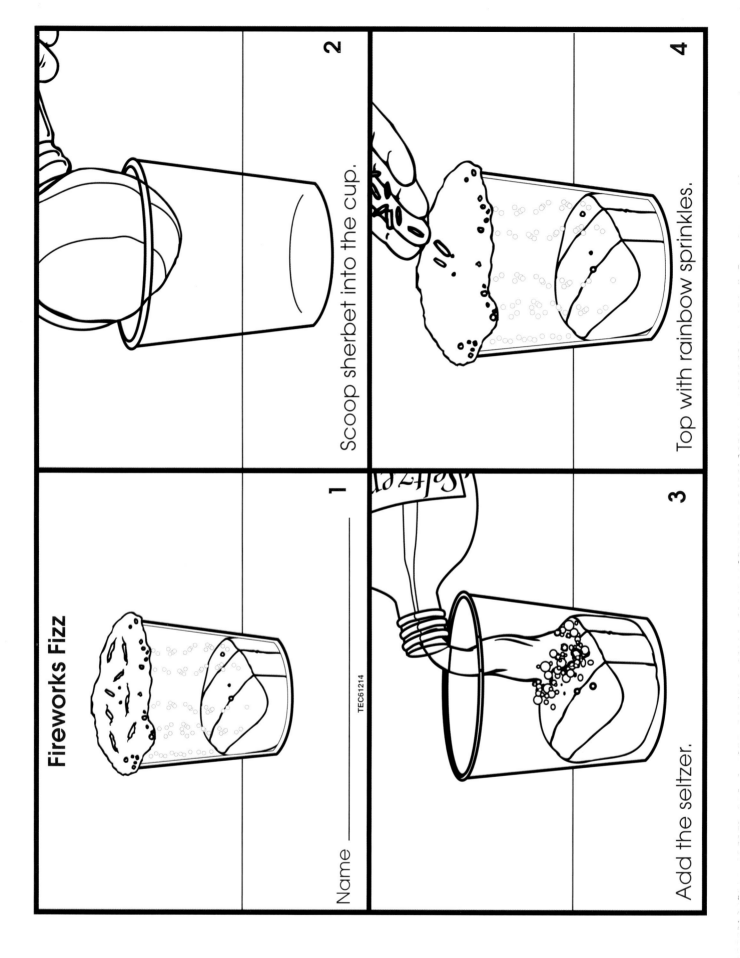

Fireworks Fizz

2 Scoop sherbet into the cup.

4 Top with rainbow sprinkles.

3 Add the seltzer.

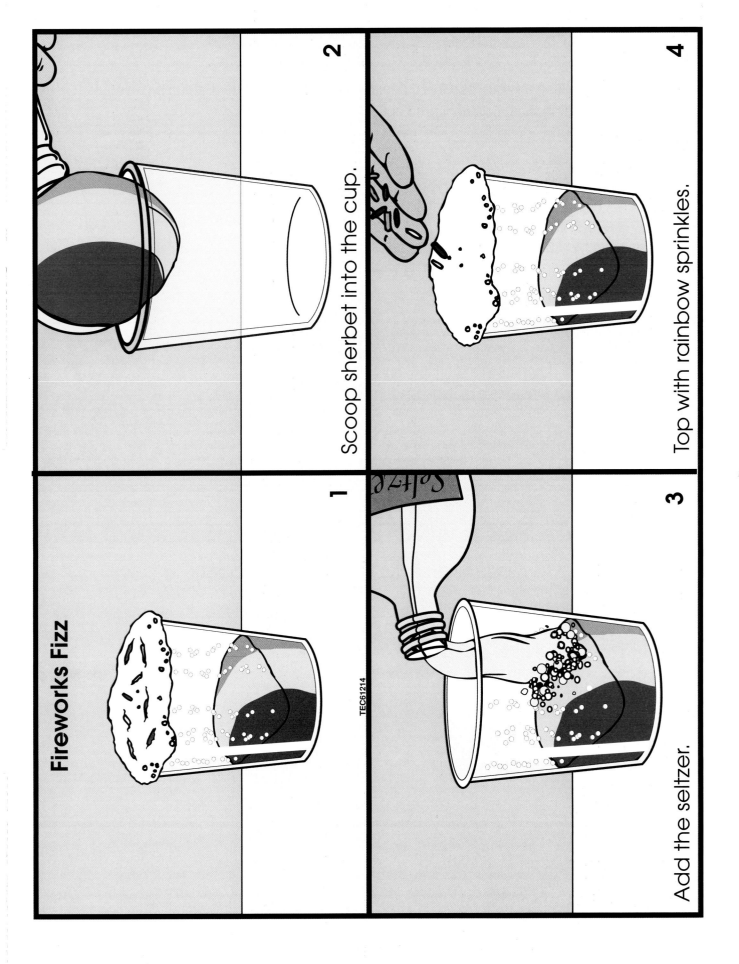

Fireworks Fizz

1

2

Scoop sherbet into the cup.

3

Add the seltzer.

4

Top with rainbow sprinkles.

Dear Parent,

   We are making a **Fireworks Fizz** snack soon. We would be grateful if you could help by providing the following ingredient(s):

_____

_____

_____

We need the ingredient(s) listed above by _____.
　　　　　　　　　　　　　　　　　　　　　　　　date

Please let me know if you are able to send the ingredient(s).

　　　　　　　　　　　　　Thank you,

　　　　　　　_____
　　　　　　　　　　　　　　　　teacher

- -

Fireworks Fizz

☐ Yes, I am able to send the ingredient(s).
☐ No, I am unable to send the ingredient(s) this time.

　　　　　　　_____
　　　　　　　　　　　　　parent signature

I Made Fireworks Fizz in School Today!

My favorite part was _____.

It tasted _____.

This is what it looked like:

Chef's signature: _____

Burger Cookie

Ingredients for one:

2 vanilla wafers (buns)
chocolate mint patty (burger)
green-tinted coconut (lettuce)
yellow-tinted frosting (mustard)
red-tinted frosting (ketchup)

Utensils and supplies:

napkin per child
2 plastic knives

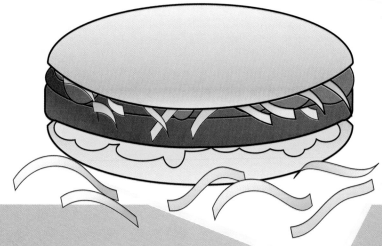

Teacher preparation:

- Arrange the supplies and ingredients for easy student access.
- Display the recipe cards from page 155. Or give each student a copy of page 154; then ask her to color and cut apart the booklet pages and staple them in order.

Susan Bunyan, Linn Elementary, Dodge City, KS

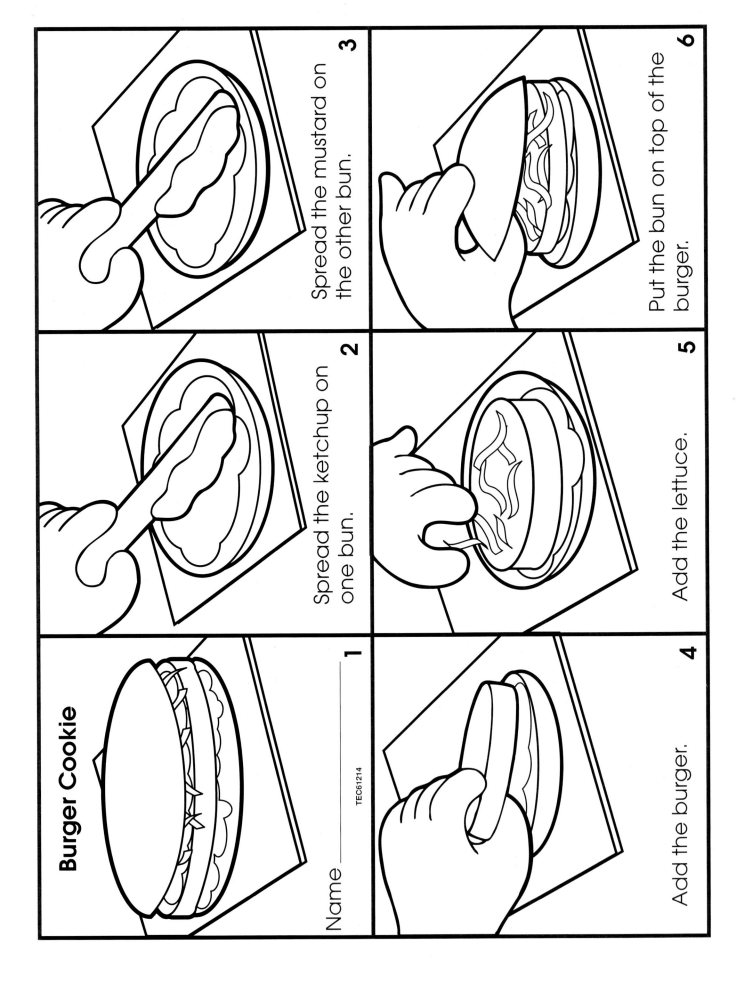

Burger Cookie

Name _____

1

2
Spread the ketchup on one bun.

3
Spread the mustard on the other bun.

4
Add the burger.

5
Add the lettuce.

6
Put the bun on top of the burger.

TEC61214

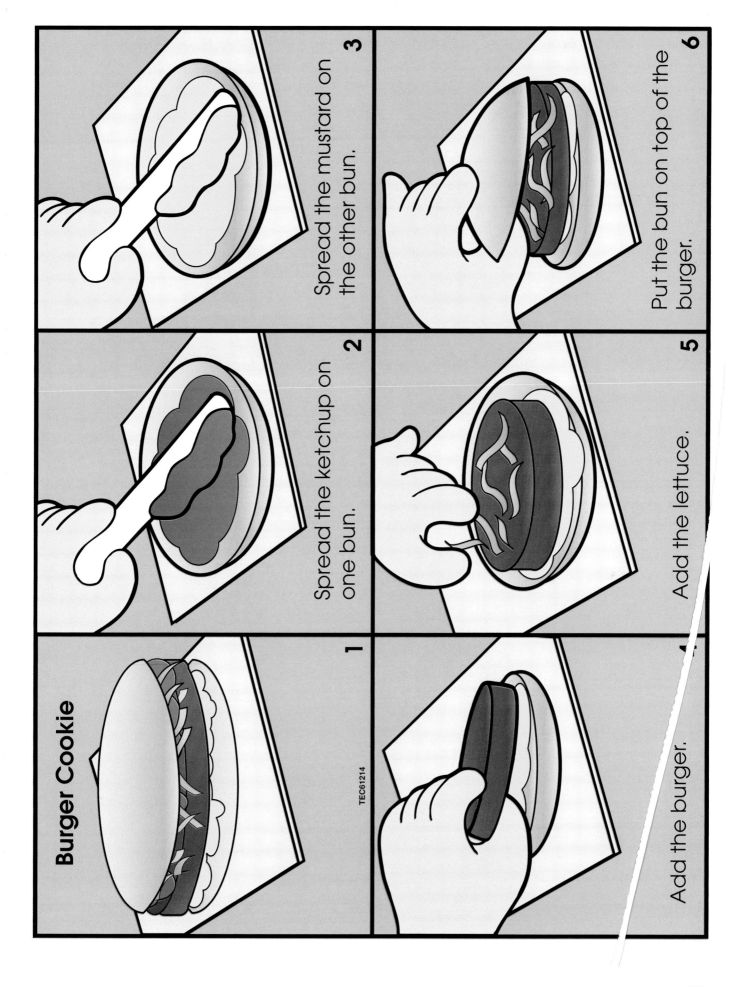

Burger Cookie

1

TEC61214

2

Spread the ketchup on one bun.

3

Spread the mustard on the other bun.

Add the burger.

5

Add the lettuce.

6

Put the bun on top of the burger.

Dear Parent,

We are making **Burger Cookies** soon. We would be grateful if you could help by providing the following ingredient(s):

_____

_____

_____

We need the ingredient(s) listed above by _____.
                                                                                      date

Please let me know if you are able to send the ingredient(s).

                            Thank you,

                        _____
                                            teacher

- -

Burger Cookies

☐ Yes, I am able to send the ingredient(s).

☐ No, I am unable to send the ingredient(s) this time.

                        _____
                                      parent signature

I Made a Burger Cookie in School Today!

My favorite part was _____.

It tasted _____.

This is what it looked like:

Chef's signature: _____

Ingredients for one:

graham cracker square
1 tbsp. whipped topping
chocolate cookie
5 mini chocolate chips

Utensils and supplies:

small paper plate for each child
measuring tablespoon
plastic knife for each child

Teacher preparation:

- Arrange the supplies and ingredients for easy student access.
- Display the recipe cards from page 159. Or give each student a copy of page 158; then ask her to color and cut apart the booklet pages and staple them in order.

adapted from an idea by Michelle Miles, Early Childhood Development Center, Charlottesville, VA

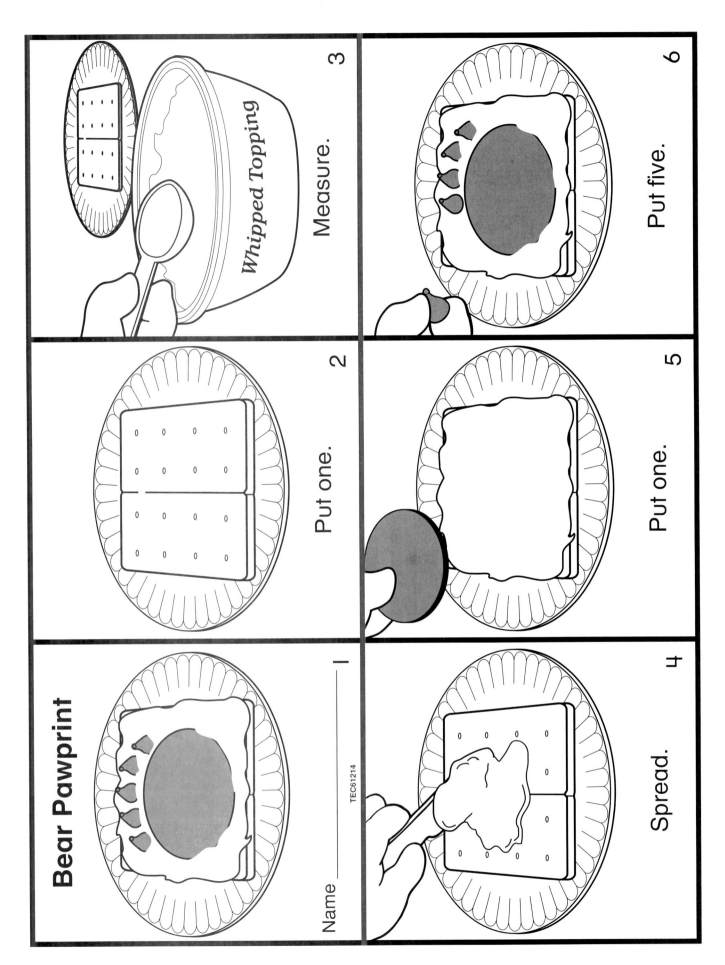

Bear Pawprint

1 _____
TEC61214

Name _____

2 Put one.

3 Measure.
Whipped Topping

4 Spread.

5 Put one.

6 Put five.

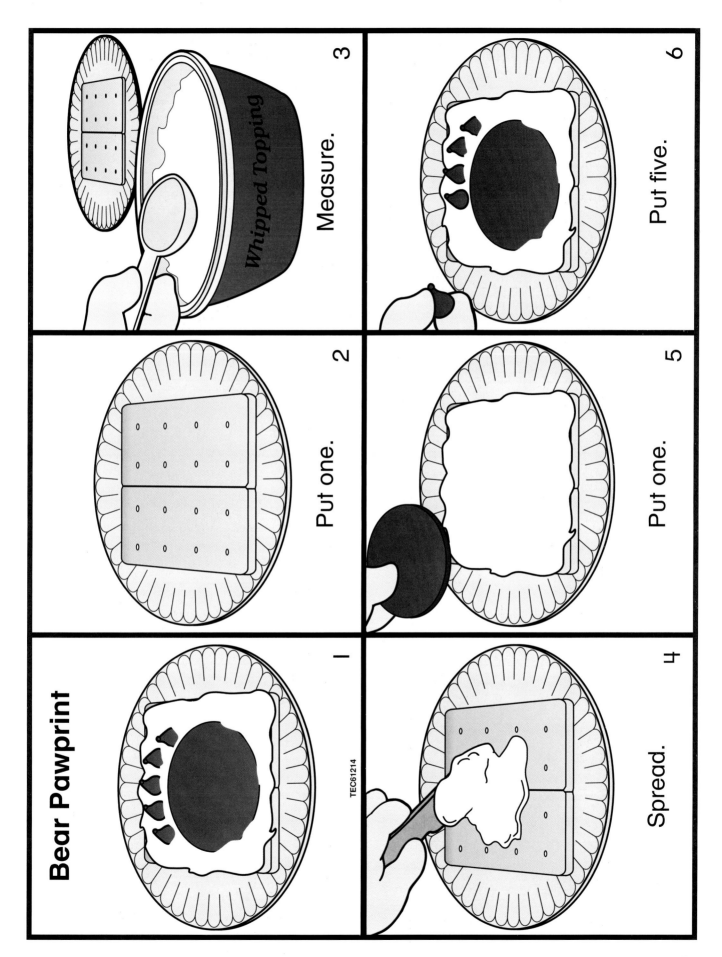

Bear Pawprint

1

2   Put one.

3   *Whipped Topping*   Measure.

4   Spread.

5   Put one.

6   Put five.

TEC61214

Dear Parent,
    We are making a **Bear Pawprint** snack soon. We would be grateful if you could help by providing the following ingredient(s):

_____

_____

_____

We need the ingredient(s) listed above by _____.
                                                      date

Please let me know if you are able to send the ingredient(s).
                    Thank you,

                    _____
                              teacher

- -

Bear Pawprint

☐ Yes, I am able to send the ingredient(s).
☐ No, I am unable to send the ingredient(s) this time.

                    _____
                              parent signature

I Made a Bear Pawprint in School Today!

My favorite part was _____.

It tasted _____.

This is what it looked like:

Chef's signature: _____

Hedgehog Biscuit

Ingredients for one:

refrigerator biscuit
pretzel sticks, broken in half
3 chocolate cereal puffs
cinnamon sugar

Utensils and supplies:

aluminum foil
baking sheet
oven
oven mitt
marker

Solomon

Teacher preparation:

- Personalize a foil square for each child.
- Arrange the supplies and ingredients for easy student access.
- Display the recipe cards from page 163. Or give each student a copy of page 162; then ask him to color and cut apart the booklet pages and staple them in order.

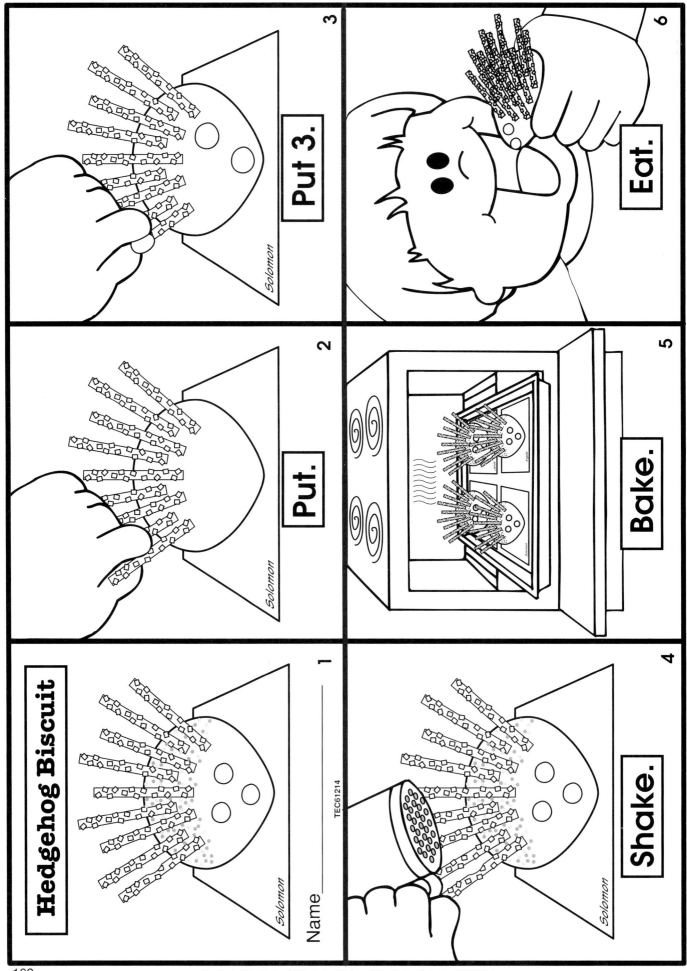

Hedgehog Biscuit

Name _____

1   Solomon

2   Solomon   **Put.**

3   Solomon   **Put 3.**

4   Solomon   **Shake.**

5   **Bake.**

6   **Eat.**

TEC61214

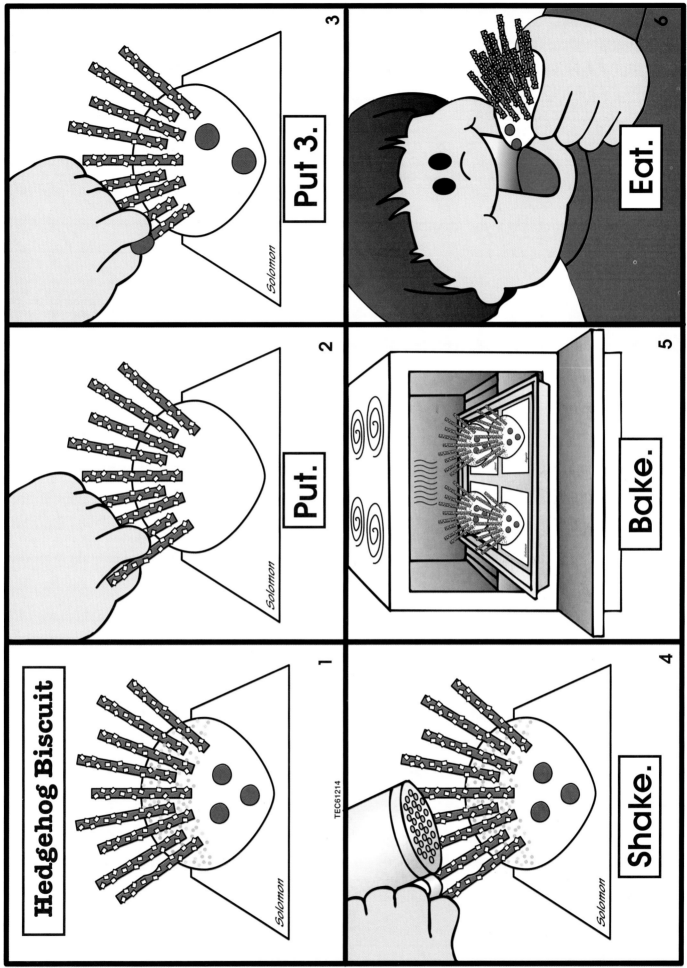

Dear Parent,

We are making **Hedgehog Biscuits** soon. We would be grateful if you could help by providing the following ingredient(s):

_____

_____

_____

We need the ingredient(s) listed above by _____.
date

Please let me know if you are able to send the ingredient(s).

Thank you,

_____
teacher

- -

Hedgehog Biscuit

☐ Yes, I am able to send the ingredient(s).

☐ No, I am unable to send the ingredient(s) this time.

_____
parent signature

I Made a Hedgehog Biscuit in School Today!

My favorite part was _____.

It tasted _____.

This is what it looked like:

Chef's signature: _____

Funny Fishbowl

Ingredients for one:

rice cake
softened cream cheese, tinted blue
rainbow sprinkles
five Goldfish crackers

Utensils and supplies:

small disposable plate for each
  child
plastic knife for each child

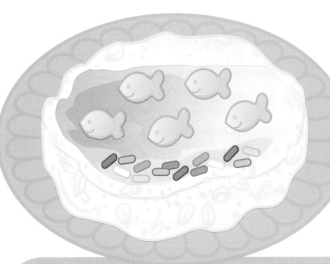

Teacher preparation:

- Arrange the supplies and ingredients for easy student access.
- Display the recipe cards from page 167. Or give each student a copy of page 166; then ask him to color and cut apart the booklet pages and staple them in order.

Cori Collins, Howe School, Green Bay, WI

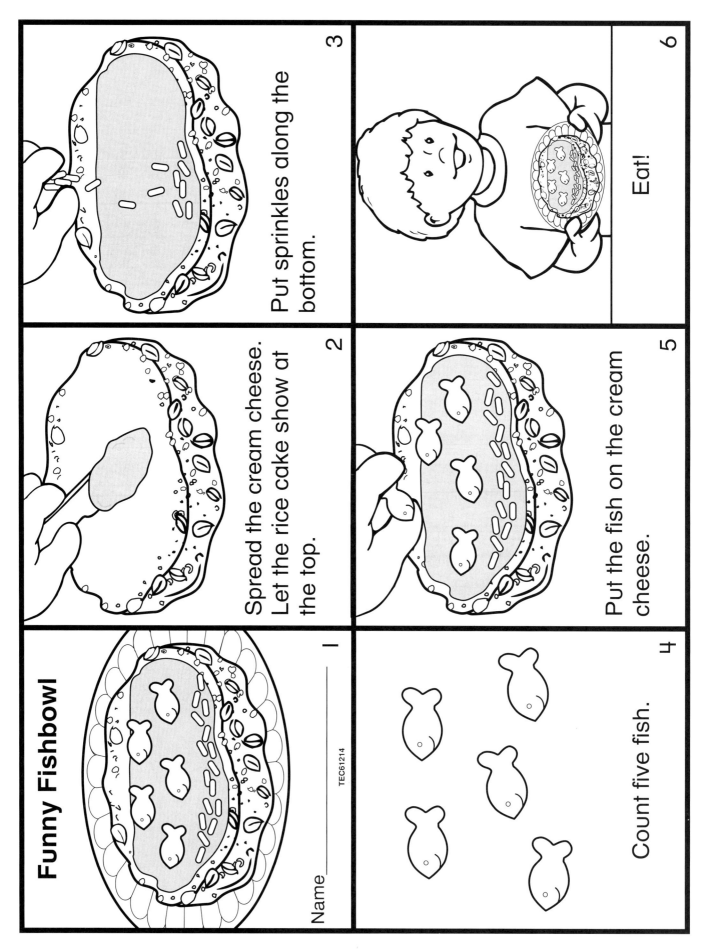

Funny Fishbowl

3. Put sprinkles along the bottom.

6. Eat!

2. Spread the cream cheese. Let the rice cake show at the top.

5. Put the fish on the cream cheese.

1.

Name _____

TEC61214

4. Count five fish.

Funny Fishbowl

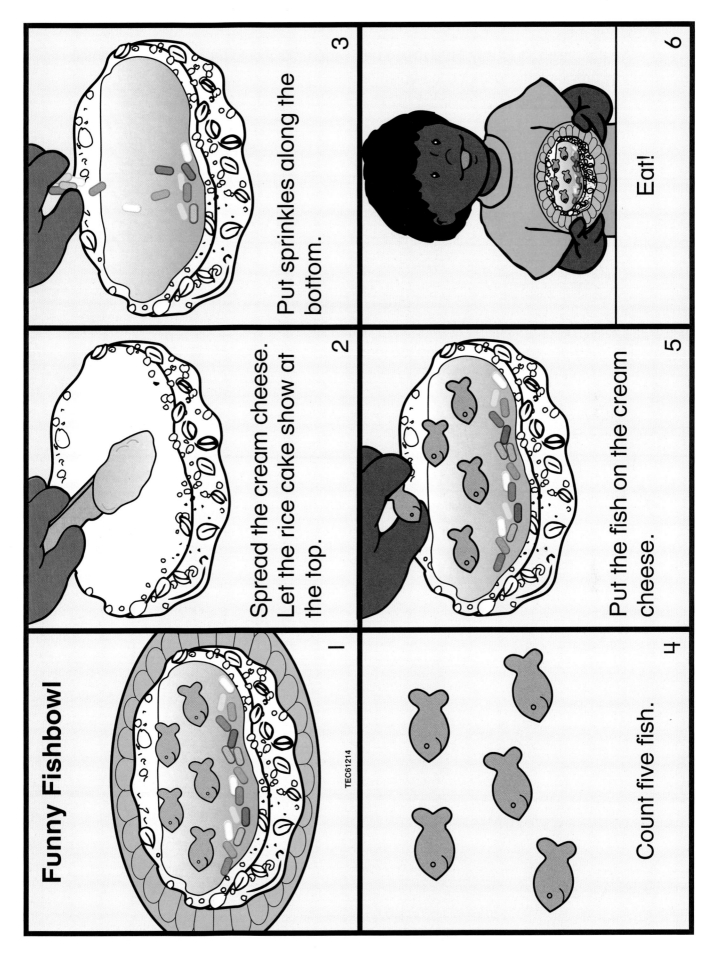

1

2 Spread the cream cheese. Let the rice cake show at the top.

3 Put sprinkles along the bottom.

4 Count five fish.

5 Put the fish on the cream cheese.

6 Eat!

TEC61214

Dear Parent,

We are making a **Funny Fishbowl** snack soon. We would be grateful if you could help by providing the following ingredient(s):

_____

_____

_____

We need the ingredient(s) listed above by _____.
date

Please let me know if you are able to send the ingredient(s).

Thank you,

_____
teacher

Funny Fishbowl

☐ Yes, I am able to send the ingredient(s).

☐ No, I am unable to send the ingredient(s) this time.

_____
parent signature

I Made a Funny Fishbowl in School Today!

My favorite part was _____.

It tasted _____.

This is what it looked like:

Chef's signature: _____

Ingredients for one:

animal cracker
Orville Redenbacher's caramel popcorn
  mini cake
1 tbsp. cold milk
1 tsp. instant chocolate pudding mix

Utensils and supplies:

plastic spoon per child
small cup per child
teaspoon
tablespoon

Teacher preparation:

- Arrange the supplies and ingredients for easy student access.
- Display the recipe cards from page 171. Or give each student a copy of page 170; then ask her to color and cut apart the booklet pages and staple them in order.

Helaine Donnelly, Washington School, Plainfield, NJ

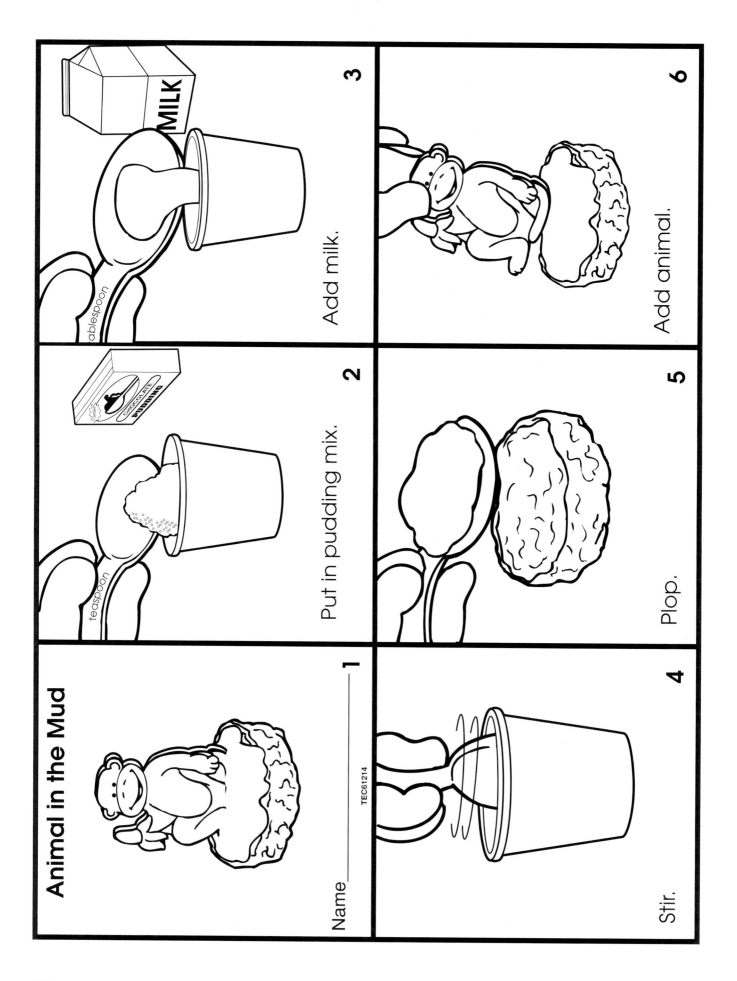

Animal in the Mud

Name _____

TEC61214

1

2
Put in pudding mix.

3
Add milk.

4
Stir.

5
Plop.

6
Add animal.

Dear Parent,

We are making an **Animal in the Mud** snack soon. We would be grateful if you could help by providing the following ingredient(s):

_____

_____

_____

We need the ingredient(s) listed above by _____.
date

Please let me know if you are able to send the ingredient(s).

Thank you,

_____
teacher

- -

Animal in the Mud

☐ Yes, I am able to send the ingredient(s).
☐ No, I am unable to send the ingredient(s) this time.

_____
parent signature

I Made an Animal in the Mud in School Today!

My favorite part was _____.

It tasted _____.

This is what it looked like:

Chef's signature: _____

Ingredients for one:

4 thin green apple slices (palm leaves)
2 sugar wafers (trunk)
3 chocolate cereal puffs (coconuts)
large spoonful of Alpha-Bits cereal

Utensils and supplies:

paper plate for each child

Teacher preparation:

- Arrange the supplies and ingredients for easy student access.
- Display the recipe cards from page 175. Or give each student a copy of page 174; then ask her to color and cut apart the booklet pages and staple them in order.

Angie Choate, Mustang Trails Elementary, Mustang, OK

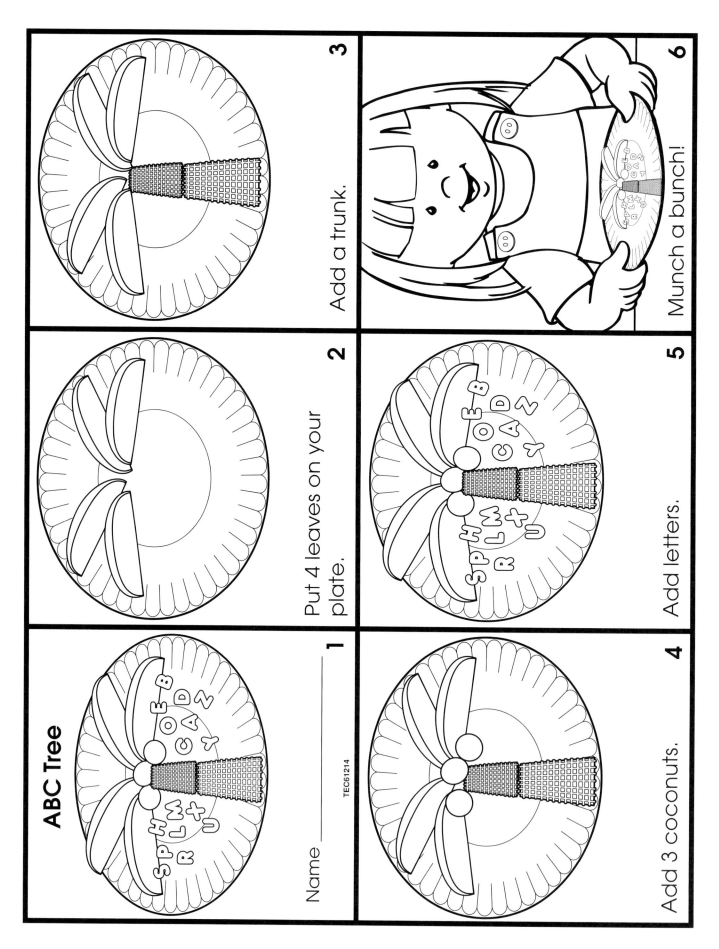

ABC Tree

Name _____

TEC61214

1

Put 4 leaves on your plate.

2

Add a trunk.

3

Add 3 coconuts.

4

Add letters.

5

Munch a bunch!

6

ABC Tree

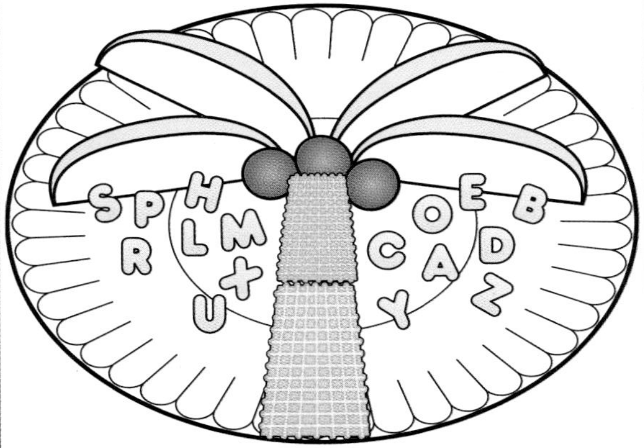

1

2

Put 4 leaves on your plate.

3

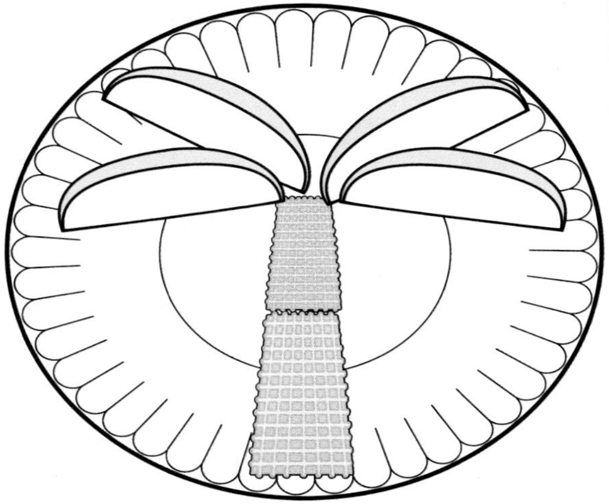

Add a trunk.

4

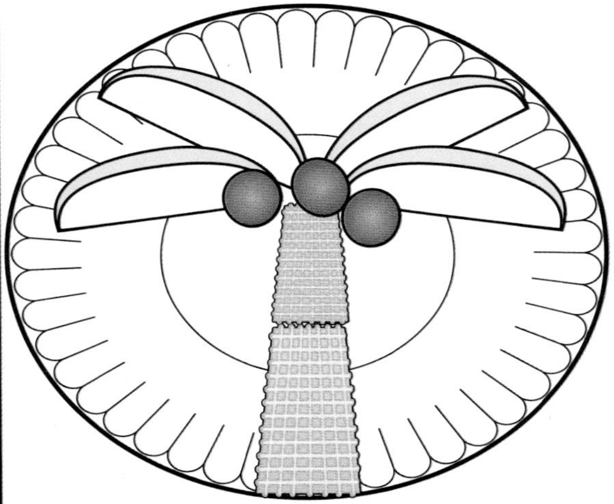

Add 3 coconuts.

5

Add letters.

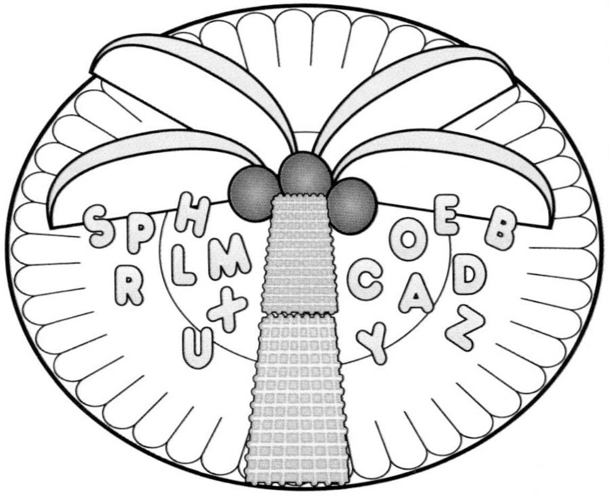

6

Munch a bunch!

TEC61214

Dear Parent,

We are making an **ABC Tree** snack soon. We would be grateful if you could help by providing the following ingredient(s):

_____

_____

_____

We need the ingredient(s) listed above by _____.

date

Please let me know if you are able to send the ingredient(s).

Thank you,

_____

teacher

- -

ABC Tree

☐ Yes, I am able to send the ingredient(s).

☐ No, I am unable to send the ingredient(s) this time.

_____

parent signature

I Made an ABC Tree in School Today!

My favorite part was _____.

It tasted _____.

This is what it looked like:

Chef's signature: _____

Tasty Train

Ingredients for one:

whole graham cracker
graham cracker square
small graham cracker square
3 thin banana slices
red decorating gel
3 oat cereal pieces

Utensils and supplies:

paper towel for each child

Teacher preparation:

- Arrange the supplies and ingredients for easy student access.
- Display the recipe cards from page 179. Or give each student a copy of page 178; then ask her to color and cut apart the booklet pages and staple them in order.

Kathy Brand, Cornerstone Christian School, New City, NY

3

Put on top.

6

Add smoke.

2

Put next to.

5

Make a window.

Tasty Train

1

TEC61214

Name _____

4

Put three wheels.

Tasty Train

1

2 Put next to.

3 Put on top.

4 Put three wheels.

5 Make a window.

6 Add smoke.

TEC61214

Dear Parent,

We are making a **Tasty Train** snack soon. We would be grateful if you could help by providing the following ingredient(s):

_____

_____

_____

We need the ingredient(s) listed above by _____.
date

Please let me know if you are able to send the ingredient(s).

Thank you,

_____
teacher

Tasty Train

☐ Yes, I am able to send the ingredient(s).

☐ No, I am unable to send the ingredient(s) this time.

_____
parent signature

I Made a Tasty Train in School Today!

My favorite part was _____.

It tasted _____.

This is what it looked like:

Chef's signature: _____

Ingredients for one:

refrigerated biscuit
margarine, melted
cinnamon sugar

Utensils and supplies:

napkin for each child
cupcake liner for each child
2 small bowls
microwave oven
baking pan
toaster oven or conventional oven

Teacher preparation:

- Arrange the supplies and ingredients for easy student access.
- Display the recipe cards from page 183. Or give each student a copy of page 182; then ask her to color and cut apart the booklet pages and staple them in order.

Susan Bresch YMCA of Burlington County Child Care Center • Mt. Laurel, NJ

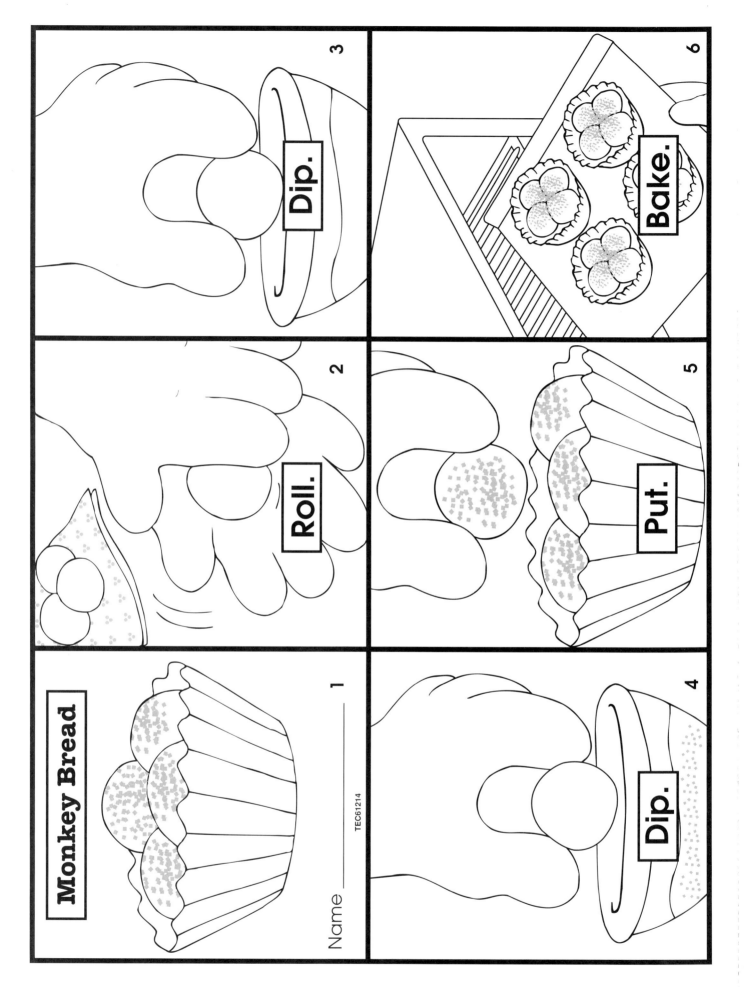

3

Dip.

6

Bake.

2

Roll.

5

Put.

Monkey Bread

1

TEC61214

Name _____

4

Dip.

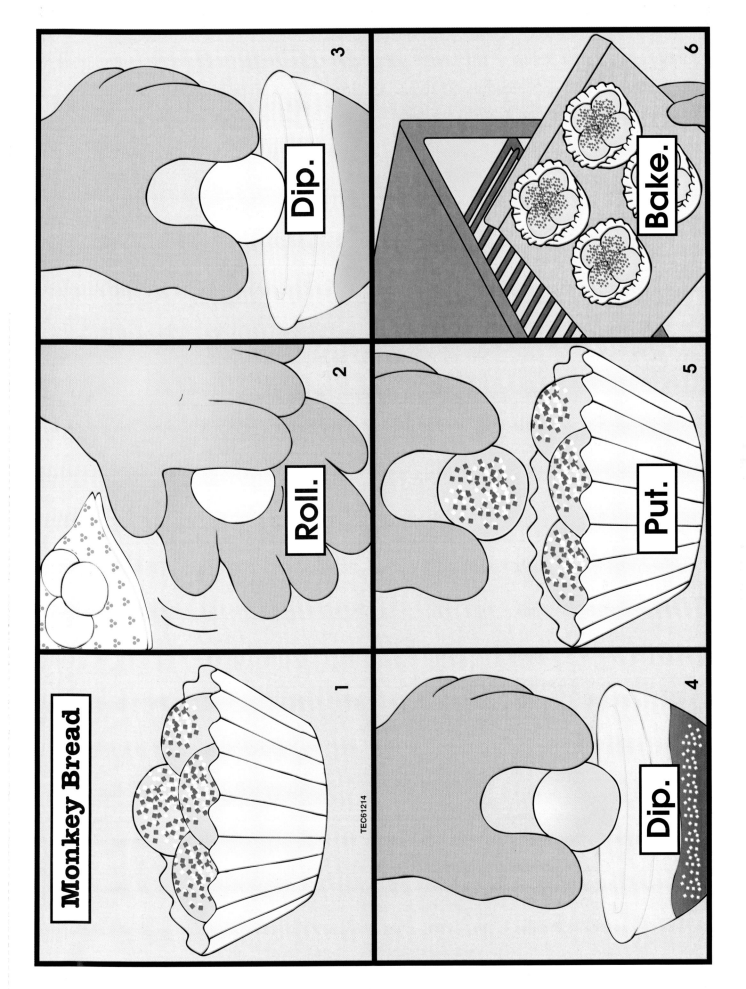

Dear Parent,

We are making a **Monkey Bread** snack soon. We would be grateful if you could help by providing the following ingredient(s):

_____

_____

_____

We need the ingredient(s) listed above by _____.
date

Please let me know if you are able to send the ingredient(s).

Thank you,

_____
teacher

Monkey Bread

☐ Yes, I am able to send the ingredient(s).

☐ No, I am unable to send the ingredient(s) this time.

_____
parent signature

I Made Monkey Bread in School Today!

My favorite part was _____.

It tasted _____.

This is what it looked like:

Chef's signature: _____

Cheese Pizza

Ingredients for one:

half of an English muffin
prepared pizza sauce
grated cheese (mozzarella and/or your
  choice)

Utensils and supplies:

spoon for each child
aluminum foil
permanent marker
hot mitt

Teacher preparation:

- Arrange the supplies and ingredients for easy student access.
- Display the recipe cards from page 187. Or give each student a copy
  of page 186; then ask him to color and cut apart the booklet pages and
  staple them in order.

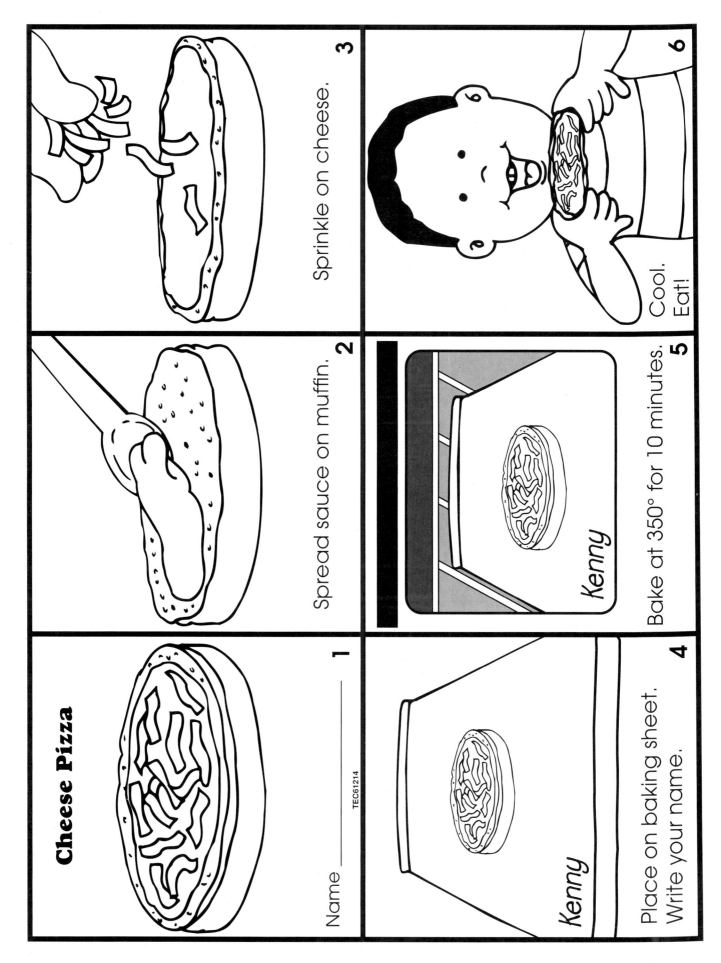

3 Sprinkle on cheese.

6 Cool. Eat!

2 Spread sauce on muffin.

5 Bake at 350° for 10 minutes.

Kenny

Cheese Pizza

1

Name _____

TEC61214

4 Place on baking sheet. Write your name.

Kenny

Cheese Pizza

1

2

Spread sauce on muffin.

3

Sprinkle on cheese.

4

Kenny

Place on baking sheet.
Write your name.

5

Kenny

Bake at 350° for 10 minutes.

6

Cool.
Eat!

TEC61214

Dear Parent,

　　We are making a **Cheese Pizza** snack soon. We would be grateful if you could help by providing the following ingredient(s):

_____

_____

_____

We need the ingredient(s) listed above by _____.
　　　　　　　　　　　　　　　　　　　　　　　　　　date

Please let me know if you are able to send the ingredient(s).
　　　　　　　　　　Thank you,

　　　　_____
　　　　　　　　　　　　　　teacher

Cheese Pizza

☐ Yes, I am able to send the ingredient(s).
☐ No, I am unable to send the ingredient(s) this time.

　　　　_____
　　　　　　　　　　　　parent signature

I Made Cheese Pizza in School Today!

My favorite part was _____.

It tasted _____.

This is what it looked like:

Chef's signature: _____

Ingredients for one:

shredded cheese (hair)
canned pear half (head)
2 mini chocolate chips (eyes)
maraschino cherry half (nose)

Utensils and supplies:

paper plate for each child
plastic fork for each child

Teacher preparation:

- Arrange the supplies and ingredients for easy student access.
- Display the recipe cards from page 191. Or give each student a copy of page 190; then ask her to color and cut apart the booklet pages and staple them in order.

Allison Pratt, Eagle Bluff Kindergarten, Onalaska, WI

3

Add 2 eyes.

6

Enjoy!

2

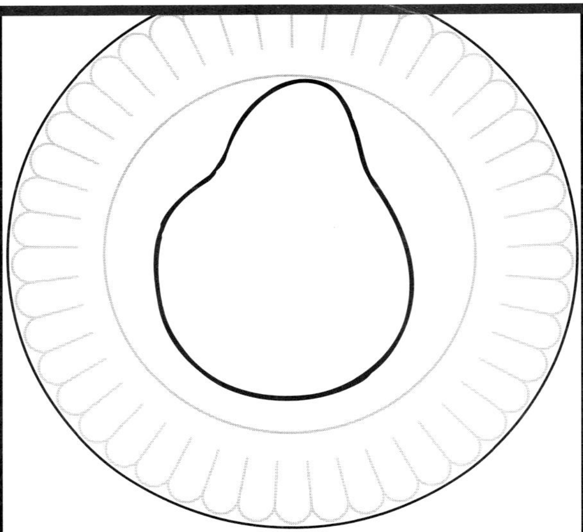

Put a pear on your plate.

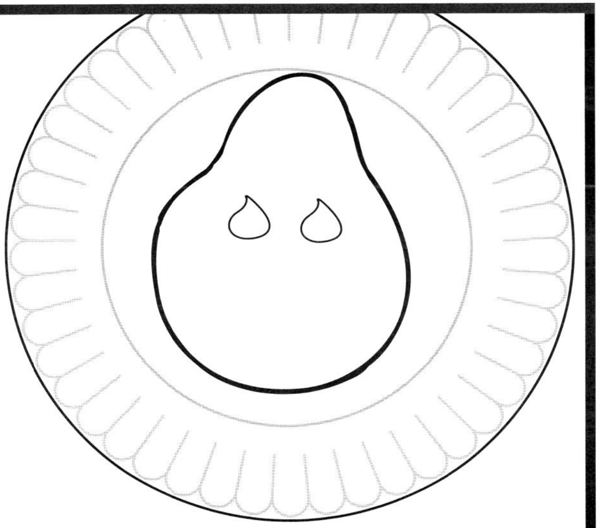

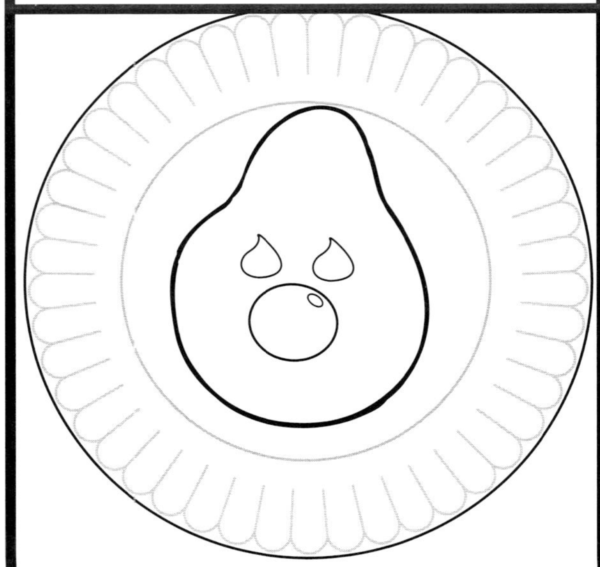

5

Add hair.

Funny Fruit Face

1

TEC61214

Name _____

4

Add 1 nose.

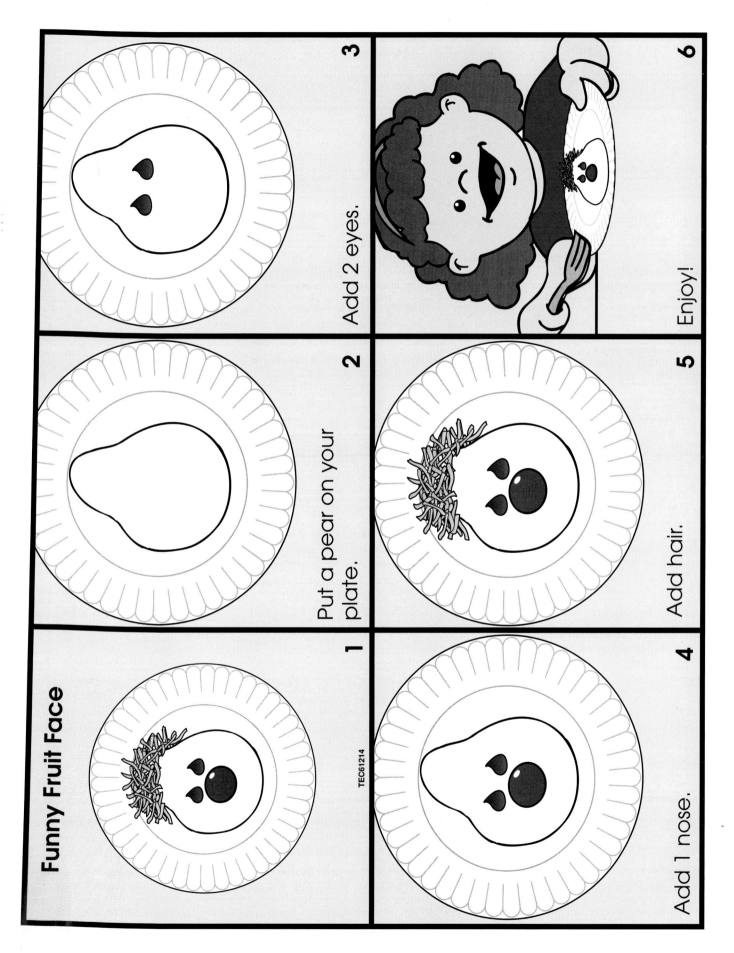

Funny Fruit Face

1

TEC61214

2

Put a pear on your plate.

3

Add 2 eyes.

4

Add 1 nose.

5

Add hair.

6

Enjoy!

Dear Parent,

We are making a **Funny Fruit Face** snack soon. We would be grateful if you could help by providing the following ingredient(s):

_____

_____

_____

We need the ingredient(s) listed above by _____.
                                                          date

Please let me know if you are able to send the ingredient(s).

Thank you,

_____
                    teacher

- -

Funny Fruit Face

☐ Yes, I am able to send the ingredient(s).
☐ No, I am unable to send the ingredient(s) this time.

_____
                 parent signature

I Made a Funny Fruit Face in School Today!

My favorite part was _____.

It tasted _____.

This is what it looked like:

Chef's signature: _____